BRINK'S, THE MONEY MOVERS

The Story of a Century of Service

A Brink's armored car on LaSalle Street, Chicago's financial center.

BRINK'S
THE MONEY MOVERS

The Story of a Century of Service

R. A. SENG

J. V. GILMOUR

PRINTED BY

The Lakeside Press

R. R. DONNELLEY & SONS COMPANY

FOREWORD

This short history, documented as fully as practicable, is published on the occasion of Brink's centennial. It is regretted that the portion dealing with the earlier years was not recorded at a time when the recollections of the founders would have amplified the somewhat incomplete records.

This is a chronicle of how a commonplace enterprise was started, how it grew along conventional lines and gradually evolved into the specialized business of transporting money and valuables by armored car which today is an integral and necessary part of modern business and banking.

It contains the annals of the Brink's men who played major roles in drawing the blueprints for expediting the movement of money under the rapidly changing conditions of the twentieth century.

For most people, money on the move has an inherent fascination. For many, this is widened by a general interest in the armored car and in the part it plays in preventing crime and securing public safety.

As president of Brink's, I have a deep conviction that armored car service is basic to modern business and that its contribution to our economy will be increasingly important in the years ahead.

Eugene E. Murphy

March 11, 1959

TABLE OF CONTENTS

CHAPTER I

A Look at the Brink's of Today

ON CHICAGO'S SOUTH SIDE at 24th Street, occupying the block between Prairie and Indiana Avenues, stands a three-story building of red brick and stone. Approaching from the east, your eye may first be caught by the slanting awnings of green glass above the wide windows of the upper floor. Crossing Prairie and gaining the sidewalk you are struck by something else—except for one small area there are no windows on the ground floor. The blank, solid expanse of the wall is broken only by a few sections of structural glass brick placed above head level of a pedestrian. A few steps farther along you discover the reason for the absence of windows: stainless steel lettering on the wall proclaims this the home of BRINK'S, INCORPORATED.

Before opening the door, you pause to watch the approach of a battleship gray armored car coming east on 24th Street. Just a few yards to the west it turns into an entry-way and pauses momentarily before steel-clad doors. The driver glances up and you do, too. What you

9

see is a bullet-proof pillbox projecting from the wall. Sitting in it is an armed guard who scans the vehicle below before pressing a button that opens the doors.

You don't know it yet, but the armored car has gone into the garage of Brink's Chicago Branch. The doorway you now enter leads into a separate entity, the general offices of the money moving company.

You step into the small lobby and immediately a rather mechanical voice addresses you with a "Yes, sir?"

Turning toward the voice you discover a cubicle protected by bulletproof glass within which sits a uniformed, armed guard who has spoken to you over an intercom. Feeling just a trifle self-conscious and awed, you tell the guard your name and business and whom you wish to see. After telephoning upstairs and obtaining clearance, your name, firm and sponsor are entered on a register and you are instructed to take the elevator to the third floor where the executive offices are located.

(*Had you been a bandit instead of a legitimate visitor, you would have learned more about the functions of the guard: that he electrically controls the all-steel doors from the lobby into the security areas of the building; that he can sound internal and outside alarm systems and summon police aid.*)

This is the nerve center of a business that, just before its 100th birthday, has 112 branches in the United States and Canada serving 2500 communities, and that operates over 1000 armored cars.

By modern standards Brink's is not a giant corporation, yet it has a peculiar impact upon the observer. It seizes the imagination because it has some of the qualities of

Fort Knox, of the Federal Reserve Banks and the United States Mints all rolled into one. For Brink's is the great money-mover of this or any other time. Its comparative handful of employes—less than five thousand all told— handle a daily average of about one and one-third *billions* of dollars in currency, coin, checks and commercial paper—more in a day than the monthly gross of giant General Motors; more in a day than the yearly gross of all but a few dozen United States companies; more in a year than the total of the national debt.

When Money Moves, Bandits Attack

If we dig back into the traceable history of mankind, we find that the very first forms of wealth were simple trade goods that were also the necessities of life—flints and salt. As the centuries rolled along, other things were added: amber from the Baltic coast, arrowheads, spears and battle axes, pottery vessels, baskets and furs. By the time the very first written records appeared, wealth—in the form of precious metals and gems—was well established as a source of luxury and of power.

Accumulated wealth was easy enough for the strong to guard. The king in his counting house running a fistful of sapphires and emeralds through appreciative fingers never worried much about robbers. However, his tax collectors bringing in gold from the provinces knew the necessity of unending vigilance against attack.

Money on the move has ever fired the imaginations of men, has aroused their lawlessness and reckless daring. For money on the move was vulnerable. It was the target for Mongol horsemen striking at the camel caravans of Asia . . . for cutthroats tracking the pilgrim bands to Canterbury . . . for the pirates of the Spanish Main such as Morgan, Dampier and Kidd . . . for privateers such as Drake raiding Cartagena under a royal patent from Queen Elizabeth I . . . for the road agents and outlaws of the American West such as Black Bart, the Plummer Gang and the James Brothers waylaying the stagecoaches and trains with their cargoes of gold.

Today, in spite of the use of checks, drafts, money orders and letters of credit, more money is on the move than ever before in history. A glance at your daily paper will convince you that there has been no decrease in lawlessness; that burglary, robbery and armed assault are commonplace against individuals and institutions alike.

Yet important accumulations of money from the United States Mints, the Federal Reserve Banks, banks and businesses flow ceaselessly along our streets and highways, and are almost never subject to attack. Why? Largely because of the armored car service which has its heart and nerve center here at Brink's.

Look around and listen in as we move through the third floor.

The president is busy with the manifold duties that occupy the head of any growing business through a long day. (Incidentally, there is a .38 revolver handy in a drawer of the president's desk as there is in the desk of each officer.) But to assay his responsibilities properly, you must imagine, if you can, the sustained pressure that bears on the chief executive of a Company dealing in something more volatile and explosive than dynamite— money. Yes, literally more than a billion dollars a day are transported over the nation's streets and highways in over a thousand armored cars, and many millions of dollars are stored overnight in over a hundred branches.

The vice president charged with purchasing is down

Main entrance to the Home Office and Chicago Branch.

in the garage inspecting a new tractor-trailer combination and analyzing the drivers' reports before the giant armored rig goes into United States Mint service hauling tons of coin to Federal Reserve Banks across the country.

The vice president in charge of business development has called in his top assistant to discuss a report on the installation of nearly two hundred Brink's Two-Key safes by Brink's Express Company of Canada, Limited; safes that are protecting the funds of two of the Dominion's larger grocery chains.

The operations vice president is setting up an over-the-weekend removal to a new building of an eastern national bank with cash and securities amounting to hundreds of millions of dollars.

Insurance rates are being analyzed for a program on which the premiums amount to more than a million dollars a year, a program so vast that it is divided among many underwriters. Labor matters are being discussed with a top official of a national union and its local representative. The accounting department is working out up-to-the-minute costs of providing service to thousands of customers under widely varying conditions. The legal staff is deep in the intricacies of filing an application for the extension of a route with a State regulatory body and the Interstate Commerce Commission. The men of Brink's must deal with all of these complexities in addition to the normal problems of wringing a reasonable profit from the gross income of a business in a competitive field.

Watching these activities, you quickly realize that this is a national institution of the broadest scope that serves not only banks, corporations, companies and individuals, but Federal, State and local governments and their numerous instrumentalities. Its activities are closely associated with law enforcement agencies and have a real bearing upon the welfare, safety and peacefulness of cities and towns. It delivers—and in many cases, disburses—thousands of payrolls each week; handles church collections and the receipts and change requirements of filling stations, chain stores, department stores, neighborhood stores, theaters, restaurants, sports arenas, race tracks and one-man businesses; safeguards not only bills and coins but the vital though uncashable cancelled checks that flow through clearing houses back to the issuing banks. Brink's is concerned with and affected by the traffic in Philadelphia; the winter condition of roads in snowy New England; the application of California laws licensing mobile check cashing installations; the growth of population throughout the United States and Canada.

The big table in the directors' room stands empty but

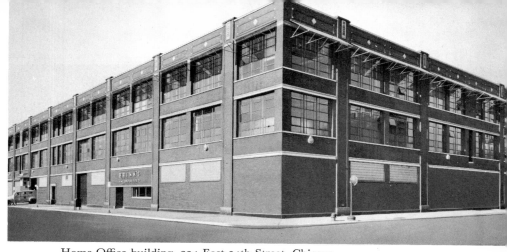

Home Office building, 234 East 24th Street, Chicago.

expectant, a pad of paper and two sharpened pencils neatly laid out before each leather upholstered chair. A meeting scheduled for two o'clock this afternoon has two major items on the docket. A discussion of improved cost-control methods. Preliminary consideration of the desirability of providing a local armored car service in a rapidly developing district where Brink's is not yet represented.

* * *

The entire first floor of the building, sealed off from the general offices by steel-clad doors, is the Chicago Branch of Brink's, Incorporated. Largest of the branches, it is none the less typical of metropolitan installations.

Here the atmosphere reflects the feeling of taut security we first encountered on entering the building. Crew members on duty are all distinctively uniformed and armed, and even the administrative and supervisory employes carry weapons constantly.

There are administration and other offices. There is a guarded room for weapons and keys from which each crewman draws his sidearms and keys as he reports for

CHAPTER II

Back to the Beginning

MAY OF 1859 was a pleasant month in Chicago. The warm spring sun was drying the mud and the dustiness of summer had not yet begun. It would have been very agreeable to sit in the sun and dream for a while, but there was no time for that.

Only twenty-six years old, Chicago had already grown to 95,000 people . . . had elbowed aside Cincinnati and St. Louis in the race for the business leadership of the raw Midwest . . . was proclaiming itself a city of destiny.

Look what the town already had! Horsecars were running south on State Street to the city limits, west on Madison and Randolph, north and northwest on Clark, Clybourn and Larrabee. Clark Street had been paved with wood blocks from Lake to Polk. And there were wooden sidewalks almost everywhere, although property owners had built these on various levels joined by stairs— some on the ground, some five or six feet in the air.

Business was booming in manufacturing, the lumber trades, milling, hides and warehousing. There were offices, banks and mercantile establishments of many kinds, restaurants, over sixty hotels and many lodging houses.

The fifty-six churches were outnumbered by eighty ball-rooms and no one knows how many saloons.

Chicago was a leading port for sailing vessels on the Great Lakes, barges plying the rivers and canals. There were railroads connecting the city with the East, and a whole new family of railroads already fanning out from Chicago into the rich hinterland south, west and north. Indeed, the steel rails were the greatest single factor in promoting the growth of this prairie metropolis.

Between the depots and Chicago's hotels moved a steady stream of travelers—a scattering of tourists out to see the West, wholesale buyers and salesmen, men of business and finance. There was a small army of drummers, including men like Marshall Field, whose heavy sample cases were packed with the goods of Cooley, Farwell and Co., Potter Palmer, and other Chicago merchants, manufacturers and jobbers.

Among the many new people in Chicago was Washington Perry Brink—Perry, to his family—an emigrant from Stockbridge, Vermont. He had a wife, Felicia, and a son, Arthur Perry, who was not yet four. Ambitious and determined but without any grandiose schemes in mind, Brink had been looking around the city for a business that promised a good living. Now, his eye caught by the steady stream of travelers, he was convinced he had found the right opportunity within reach of his modest capital.

Simply by purchasing a sound horse and light wagon he was in business. If the wagon was a new one, his investment may have been about two hundred dollars; if a used one, as little as one hundred. The lettering on the sides of the wagon read, "Brink's City Express" and his job was to transport trunks and carpet bags, traveling

Section of a large painting recreating the scene at the original Brink's office. Painted in 1949 by Theodore E. Frazee, now manager of the Kansas City Branch. There are no known photos of Brink's vehicles prior to 1900 though the Company owned about 85 wagons and over 200 horses at the turn of the century.

boxes and sample cases, even to do light draying for the merchants in town. It was the fifth of the month when he made his first trip.

It is likely that Perry Brink was attracted to the express business by the success attained by several pioneer expressmen such as Henry Wells, William G. Fargo and Alvin Adams. Wells and Adams were fellow Vermonters, and Wells had founded the American Express Company in 1850. Adams, with other associates, organized The Adams Express Company in 1854. Wells, also in association with Fargo, organized Wells Fargo and Company in 1852. The business of all three companies was primarily "to move packages, money and valuables."

By 1859 these three expanding companies were doing

a business amounting to millions of dollars a year. American and Adams dominated the East, Wells Fargo the West. They were among the glamorous growth businesses of the era. Even giving Perry Brink credit for high aspirations, it is unlikely he ever imagined his modest enterprise would one day be the outstanding leader in the moving of money and valuables.

Business was good from the start and soon got even better. In May of 1860 Chicago was chosen by the new Republican party as the site of its first convention to be held at the Wigwam. Politicos, delegates and reporters flocked into town. It is probable that Perry Brink delivered to the Richmond Hotel the trunks of Seward and his delegates, to the Tremont House the carpet bag of Abe Lincoln, in on the Springfield train.

In these early days, Brink had no thought of money moving but, unofficially, he did some nevertheless. It was surprising how frequently a traveler refused to be separated from his luggage on the short trip from station to hotel or lodging house. Perry knew from the heft of the bag that it must have contained a small hoard of the "hard" money then so much in favor. Well, it made no difference. Trunk or bag, it still put silver in his pocket.

Perry had no need for an office as yet. With Yankee thrift he operated from his living quarters. First on South Street near Halsted, later from 215 Kinzie Street, then from 62 Whiting which is now North State.

It must be assumed that the Civil War did not affect Brink's venture adversely. Very soon he found himself called upon to transfer more trunks and packages than he could handle alone. That meant more horses, more wagons and some helpers.

Hiring helpers gave another opportunity to exercise

Vermont shrewdness. Brink hired only single men and then required them to board with him. This little side-line enabled him to kill several birds with one stone. It recovered part of the money paid out in wages. And it enabled him to keep close tab on his men. Since office and home were the same address, there was no excuse for not finishing the day's run. There were no wives to lay down the law about being home for an early supper. This meal was served at the boarding house whenever the men came in.

It is interesting to note that the "Company Boarding House" was continued for several decades, even after office and living quarters were separated and Perry Brink was dead.

From the earliest days, Brink made no effort to super-vise the morals or off-duty activities of his employes. Then, as now, the first requirement was honesty. Beyond that, Perry asked only courtesy on the job, willingness and a strong back.

All of Brink's men were husky, some have become legendary for their feats of strength. Until recent years, old timers loved to talk about Simon Nelson and his helper. This monumental pair frequently toured the neighborhood saloons of a summer evening. When they found a spot where the brewery wagon was making a delivery, Nelson would offer to bet the bystanders that he and his helper could lift the wagon with its load of barrels. The neighborhood "regulars" knew better than to wager, but strangers were usually quick to cover the bet. One at each end of the wagon, Nelson and his pal would lift it six inches off the street, set it down gently, collect the money and look for another victim.

* * *

1871—State and Madison. Just two blocks away at the northeast corner of State and Randolph, Brink's downtown office was destroyed. After the fire, Brink's returned to the same location at 39 Randolph Street.
Chicago Tribune photo.

According to "Moving Money" by Forrest Crissey, published in 1929, it was in 1868 that Brink first opened a business office separate from his home. The Chicago city directory for that year gives the address as 39 Randolph Street. It was here that the well-known Brink's blackboard first appeared. Passing customers, or their messengers, could chalk instructions for the pick-up and delivery of trunks and parcels.

Because Brink left no written records, we must rely on handed-down stories for what happened to the young company during the Great Chicago Fire of October 1871. The office at State and Randolph, and the boarding house were destroyed, but the horses and wagons made it possible to carry furniture and personal possessions beyond the reach of the flames that left the heart of the city a charred and smoking rubble. As virile Chicago sprang back to life with a furious surge of energy, Brink's City Express was on hand to help with the job.

Brink's Is Formally Organized

During the next decade changes came rapidly. The most important occurred late in this period when Perry Brink died and the affairs of the company were left in the hands of Arthur Perry Brink who had joined his father in 1873 at the age of eighteen.

In spite of his youth, "A.P." was a capable and far-sighted businessman. His associates of later years describe him as brisk, lively and energetic. He believed that Brink's City Express had a bright future which could be achieved more rapidly by incorporating the company, strengthening its financial position and interesting men of influence in the business.

On February 8, 1879 the Secretary of State authorized J. J. Luther, B. Schermerhorn, A. P. Brink and J. H. Bradley to open a book of subscriptions to capital stock of Brink's Chicago City Express Company. Each man subscribed to 20 shares at $100 per share. The four made up the board of directors and the first officers were Schermerhorn, president; Brink, vice president; Bradley, secretary; Luther, treasurer. Luther also served as superintendent with Brink as assistant.

Why did this particular group unite to incorporate Brink's? For a simple and practical reason. Schermerhorn and Bradley had connections with two large express companies operating over thousands of miles of railways and serving many cities. But deliveries in Chicago by such inter-city agencies were limited to the downtown district.

Brink's had no such restrictions. It could complement the others—and be aided by them—in handling packages, trunks and merchandise to be picked up or delivered in the outlying city and suburban areas.

BELL TELEPHONE COMPANY,

❧ PROPRIETORS ❧

Chicago Telephonic Exchange.

(*Licensed under Alex. Graham Bell's Patents*)

CENTRAL OFFICE: No. 125 LA SALLE STREET.

OPEN DAY AND NIGHT.

TO CALL THE CENTRAL OFFICE, turn the crank on the bell strongly, at the same time pressing upwards the knob on the bottom. The call will be answered by the ringing of your bell. Then turn the switch to the right hand button and use your telephone.

When you are called from the Central Office, answer by ringing your bell the same number of times as your call, *i. e.*, if your call is three, answer three; then turn the switch to the right and use your telephone. Speak clearly and distinctly, with your lips gently TOUCHING the telephone. When you have finished, turn the switch back to the left and hang the telephone on the hook provided on the bell. In requesting connections with other subscribers, first give the name of your own firm, then the name and location of parties wanted. *While waiting for the connection to be made, turn your switch to the left, and as soon as the parties desired are connected on your wire the operator at Central Office will ring your bell once as a signal that the connections are made.*

When you have finished, hang the telephone on the designated hook, turn the switch to the left and ring the bell ONCE as a signal for the Central Office to disconnect wires.

Subscribers are requested to report promptly to this office any trouble with wires or instruments.

Messengers Furnished Promptly from the Central Office.

November 1, 1878.   H. H. ELDRED, GENERAL MANAGER.

↦ LIST OF SUBSCRIBERS. ↤

WIRE.	CALL.	
		A
706	4	ABBOTT, A. A., Beach and Sebor sts.
204	2	ADAMS EXPRESS CO., 53 Madison st.
5	5	ALLERTON PACKING CO., 95 Washington st.
190	4	ANDERSON, J. A., 65 E. Indiana st.
715	2	ANDERSON, F. A., Jackson st., near Canal st.
114	5	ARMSTRONG & CO., 246 Lake st.
18	5	ARMSBY, J. K., 22-24 River st.
18	2	ARNOLD, CHAS. L., & CO., 98 S. Water st.
		B
6	2	BALTIMORE & OHIO, 83 Clark st.
210	4	BARNHARDT, BROS. & SPINDLER, 146 5th ave.
165	2	BAUER, JULIUS & CO., 263-265 Wabash ave.
22	3	BARRETT, M. L., 38 Dearborn st.
89.	4	BARRETT, ARNOLD & KIMBALL, 156 Lake st.
83	2	BARRETT, ARNOLD & KIMBALL, Goose Island.
526	2	BACH, E., Ashland ave. and 22d st.
89	2	BAEDER, ADAMSON & CO., 182 Lake st.
543	2	BATESON, ALEXANDER, 22d and Lumber sts.
152	3	BAKER & CO., 184 S. Clark st.
712	4	BASSETT, N. B., 105 So. Canal st.
513	2	BEIDLER, J. & BROS., Loomis and 22d sts.
		, BELL TELEPHONE CO. GENERAL OFFICE, 125 La Salle st.
		BELL TELEPHONE CO. BRANCH OFFICE, Halsted st.
		BELL TELEPHONE CO. BRANCH OFFICE, Canal st.

WIRE.	CALL.	
		B—Continued.
		BELL TELEPHONE CO. BRANCH OFFICE, N. Clark st.
185	2	BENT, GEO. P., 81 Jackson st.
79	2	BENNETT, HERBERT E., 162 Washington st.
501	2	BIGELOW BROS., Fisk and 22d sts.
131	2	BICKFORD, KNOX & CO., 230 So. Water st.
707	2	BLAKE, WALKER & CO., 24-26 N. Clinton st.
707	4	BLATCHFORD, E. W. & CO., Clinton and Fulton.
200	2	BLOMGREEN BROS., 162-164 S. Clark st.
186	2	BLOCH & ARNSTEIN, 176-178 Adams st.
113	4	BOWEN, H. S., 86 S. Market st.
155	2	BOONE, Dr. L. D., 133 La Salle st.
25	5	BOOTH, A., 63 Lake st.
39	5	BOWEN & LESTER, 57 Lake st.
169	4	BRACHVOGEL, CHAS., 261 Wabash ave.
110	2	BROWN, GEO. E. & CO., 12 La Salle st.
195	2	BROWN, S. A. & CO., Room 7, 234 So. Water st.
702	2	BRADSHAW, F. M., 280 Centre ave.
18	4	BRADSHAW & WAIT, 18-20 River st.
21	4	BRINTNALL, LAMB & CO., 78-80 Lake st.
41	4	BROOKS & NEEMES, 36-38 Michigan ave.
53	3	BRYANT & STRATTON, 77-81 State st.
69	2	BRUNSWICK, J. M. BALKE & CO., 47-49 State st.
68	3	BRUNSWICK, J. M. BALKE & CO., Rush, cor Kinzie
58	2	BRINK'S EXPRESS, 39 Randolph st.
132	3	BRADNER SMITH & CO., 119 Monroe st.
		BRAND, E. L., 210-212 Wabash ave.

Page from the Chicago Telephone Directory, November 1878.

The Company was one of the original telephone subscribers and thus was directly connected by phone with more than 500 of Chicago's leading firms and business

An advertising card used by Brink's in the 'eighties. Diagram on the back marks delivery limits.

men. Additional equipment was purchased and the services began to be advertised. A card from this period is reproduced here.

Studying the corporate records of the period, it is apparent that Luther and Brink were the active operating heads of the Company. When Luther died in 1886, Brink succeeded him as superintendent and then moved up to the title of manager.

However, the four-man board of directors retained tight financial control. They passed on such items as the expenditure of $10 for remodeling a light delivery wagon, purchasing a horse for $50 and a used wagon for $25. The Company prospered under this regime. Generous and regular dividends were paid. So generous that when Fred Luther wished to resign and sell the stock inherited from his father, the board of directors paid him $4200 for the twenty shares—and promptly resold five of them to Alonzo Wygant for $2100 at a profit of 100%! Wygant, also associated with a major express company, replaced Luther as a director.

The minutes of the corporate meetings, brief as they are, contain many entries that are interesting, surprising or nostalgic to modern eyes.

1880—Consider adopting a uniform. Take inventory, wagons and harness. Cash $2512.10.

1881—Inventory of stock and properties requested; also statement of expenses and revenues from company boarding house. Authority to buy 12 horses to replace losses from prevalent horse disease.

1882—For better protection of the Company's wagons on the streets of the city, the Supt. be instructed to hire a boy to ride on certain wagons that deliver trunks and valuable matter. Salaries paid shall not exceed $10 per month for each boy.

There is an interesting sidelight in this connection. In "The Romance of Moving Money" (1934), a story is told about one driver who said, "I don't want no wagon boy. Got a better one than any you can furnish," and pointing to a bow-legged, battle-scarred English bull, went on to say, "He's worth ten two-legged wagon boys when it comes to taking care of packages, but I don't expect him to draw but a boy's wages." The dog went on the payroll at $3 a week and for many years gave his owner's wagon perfect protection against attempted theft.

In 1890, the April quarterly statement showed a balance of $9,309. Expenditures were itemized as follows:

		Sundries were:	
Horse shoeing. . . $	521.60		
Sundries.	522.92		
Help.	10,921.29		
Advertising.	505.28	Painting wagons. . . . $	64.50
Barn	2,015.71	Hired teams.	22.14
Fuel	195.57	Lawyers fees.	22.00
New stock.	927.50	Detective.	4.00
Medicine.	14.50	Insurance.	208.00
Repairs.	523.54	Rope.	20.38
Rents.	1,220.98	Telephones.	132.40
Stationery.	151.18	Checks.	28.00
Loss.	137.57	Safe.	21.50
	$17,657.64		$522.92

In 1890 after many discussions, a 99-year lease was signed for a 100 x 189 foot lot at 132 W. Monroe Street, afterwards numbered 711 W. Monroe Street, on which a stable and warehouse building was to be constructed to cost not less than $30,000.00. The office remained at 88 Washington Street, and capital stock of the Company was increased to $75,000.00

Many purchases were made of wagons and teams . . . ten wagons were bonded to handle customs house goods . . . an offer was rejected to buy the Wabash Avenue property occupied by the notorious Libby Prison of Civil War days which had been moved from Richmond, Virginia to Chicago . . . a building was rented in Englewood on the south side . . . the general office was moved from 88 Washington to better quarters on the first floor of 84 Washington.

And there were two particular entries, each of special

Horse and wagon traffic at railroad station in the 1860's.
Courtesy of the Metropolitan Museum of Art.

significance. In March, 1891, the directors moved to have the Company bond its own men exclusive of hostlers. The men were to be charged 50¢ per month until the $5 annual cost had been paid; at the expiration of the year, each man still employed would be refunded all but 15% of his payment. In December, 1897 the Board of Directors approved the action of the manager and superintendent in arranging for delivery of payrolls as per the list on file.

In these two entries there is the first suggestion of an idea and a service that was to shape the future destiny of Brink's Chicago City Express Company. An idea that pointed the way to the movement of money and valuables as an increasingly important and ultimately the sole function of the Company; an idea that contained the germ of the entire armored car industry of today.

CHAPTER III

Money on the Move

BRINK'S, MERELY as a mover of goods and packages, holds little interest for the modern reader beyond the nostalgic and antiquarian values implicit in its hundred years of history. But Brink's, as the originator of many services having to do with the moving of money and valuables, has a far more compelling appeal.

It is possible—perhaps even probable—that back in the days of Perry Brink the young company may have transported cash for one or more of the handful of Chicago banks then in existence, but there is no written record of such a service.

In "Moving Money" however, it is recorded that the first payroll delivery was made to the plant of the Western Electric Company in 1891. This is substantiated by the fact, as noted at the conclusion of the preceding chapter, that the directors of the Company moved to bond their drivers in this same year.

In the spring of 1893, The World's Columbian Exposition opened in Chicago with the then revolutionary "White City" built on the Midway. Brink's was authorized to deliver parcels and express packages in the Expo-

Looking down the basin at Chicago's World's Columbian Exposition, 1893.
Chicago Historical Society photo.

sition grounds. Old timers have reported its spic and span wagons with picked teams also transported bags of the souvenir "Columbian" half dollars, and became a familiar sight to countless visitors.

In this same year the financial panic of 1893–4 began. It hit Chicago hard with tens of thousands jobless, some even starving, and with rioting of such proportions that it was necessary to quell it with troops. Brink's business suffered but not to a degree that in any way threatened the survival of the Company.

Several money-moving contracts such as the letter of agreement reproduced on the following page still exist in Brink's archives. In August, 1905, the Company agreed to call twice monthly at the Corn Exchange National Bank, Adams and LaSalle Streets, pick up a payroll not to exceed $12,000 and deliver it to the factory of the Chicago Ornamental Iron Company at 37th St. and Stewart Ave. The charge for this service was to be $5.00 per trip.

A similar agreement was drawn in 1908 with Joseph T. Ryerson & Son. This called for a weekly pick-up at

Capital $75,000⁰⁰

84 WASHINGTON ST.

ESTABLISHED 1859

STORAGE WAREHOUSES AND OFFICE.
132-138 W. MONROE ST.

Chicago, Ill. Aug. 10, 1904.

Memorandum of agreement between Brink's C. C. Express Co. and Devoe & Raynolds Co.

Brink's C. C. Express Co. agree to call at the office of Devoe & Raynolds Co., 176 Randolph St., Chicago, Ill. on or about 4 P. M., Friday of each week, receipt for and get sealed pay-roll and deliver same in like condition to the factory of Devoe & Raynolds Co., 400 N. Halsted St., on or about 4.30 P. M. same day. Brink's C. C. Express Co. to assume responsibiltiy of safe delivery of said pay-roll up to the amount of $1,000.

For the above service Devoe & Raynolds Co. agree to pay the said Brink's C. C. Express Co. $2.00 per trip. This contract to go into effect Friday, Aug. 12, 1904 and may be cancelled by either party, by giving 30 days written notice.

Signed   **BRINK'S CHICAGO CITY EXPRESS CO.**

DEVOE & RAYNOLDS CO.

Signed

The decorative "gay nineties" letterhead portrays the huge cannonball that stood in front of the 84 Washington Street office for many years, and became as much of a landmark as was the famous blackboard of earlier days. The ball, still in Brink's possession, was one of the 425-pound shot for the 15-inch guns of the U. S. ironclad *Passaic* during the Civil War.

the Merchant's Loan & Trust Co., Adams & Clark Sts., and delivery of a $3,500 payroll to 16th and Campbell. Also for the twice monthly delivery of a $6,500 payroll. For both services, Brink's was to receive $4.00 per week.

In a 1909 contract Brink's agreed to call twice monthly at the Colonial Trust and Savings Bank for a payroll up to $7,000 and deliver it to the Union Wire Mattress Company at Blackhawk and Cherry. The fee for this was three dollars per delivery.

Any business man reading the costs of these services is almost bound to come up with an incredulous whistle. They were indeed low, even considering that the dollar had something like six to eight times its present purchasing power. (Witness the fact that Brink's could provide an extra laborer for household moving at 25¢ an hour.) Yet it is true that today's armored car, costing many times as much as a horse and wagon, manned by a highly trained crew and insured for $15,000,000, in effect makes a delivery for a substantially lower real cost.

Not just the times, but the conditions have changed. At the turn of the century, Chicago had its share of violence and crime, mostly in the form of street brawling, petty thievery and burglary. Armed robbery was rare and organized banditry was unknown except in what was left of the "Wild West."

The delivery of money by Brink's followed the patterns established in the middle of the nineteenth century by such pioneers as William F. Harnden, "the father of Express," L. B. and D. B. Earle, Alvin Adams, Henry Wells, William G. Fargo, John Butterfield and Crawford Livingston. These men, or their messengers, carried money and valuables in ordinary carpet bags and traveled by private vehicle, stage coach, rail or steamboat

Brink's in 1892 at 132 West Monroe Street (later 711). J. D. Allen once wrote concerning this picture: "I started as a wagon boy—like those lads you see in the front row. The men with uniform caps that look like street car motormen's caps are Messengers. The dressed up gent at the far right looking sort of pompous and proud is A. P. Brink, son of Perry. The dapper man on the far left with his hand on his hip is William B. Wyne, who was Treasurer for many years. Can you spot the powerful lad who bet one of the boys a dollar he could lift a 50-gallon barrel of molasses over the tailgate of a wagon, carry it to a platform and back to the wagon without putting it down? He won the bet. Not such a great feat, you say? You'll think so when I tell you he had only one arm!"

as was required. Messengers looked like any other travelers and rarely encountered difficulties when moving about the country.

A Brink's man picking up money usually wrapped it loosely in a pair of overalls or a newspaper, and put it under the seat of the wagon. If the sum was a large one, a shotgun was also under the seat. Inconspicuousness was evidently regarded as the prime element in safety.

W. H. Turney, a superintendent of Brink's, was quoted in "The Romance of Moving Money" as saying:

> "Every railroad entering Chicago from the West and Southwest was strung with grain elevators which were well outside the city—and they all had to have liberal quantities of cash. This was also true of large manufacturing plants. It was my regular practice to slip into a downtown bank and pick up a payroll of five to ten thousand dollars wrapped in a newspaper or tucked in a workman's tool kit, board a Rock Island train to 63rd Street, there hire a horse and buggy and then drive miles out into the country through a desolate and almost uninhabited region.
>
> I was careful to dress in old and often disreputable clothes, and the horse and buggy which I hired looked equally disreputable . . . Fear? I never knew a moment of anxiety! . . . Today I can hardly credit the sense of perfect security I felt on those country trips—and all others, for that matter."

W. B. Wyne, superintendent when A. P. Brink was manager, is authority for the statement that he usually made money deliveries in Chicago with a small, one-horse buggy exactly like hundreds of others on the streets. (The minutes of a directors' meeting for October 1906 include a motion to purchase two "democrat buggies" for delivering money.) Mr. Wyne said that the same shells remained in his sawed-off shotgun year after year.

Where were the bandits, the bank robbers, the organ-

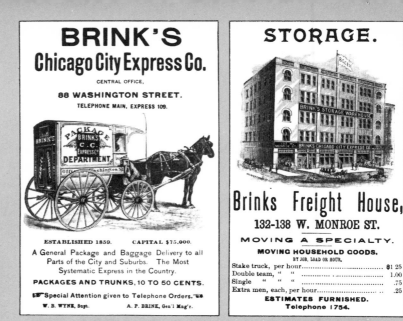

ized gangsters, the "syndicates" that should have preyed happily upon such an innocent and almost unprotected traffic in substantial sums of cash? Even the depression of the mid-nineties that threw thousands out of work and precipitated a wave of petty crime failed to result in the recorded hold-up of a single Brink's wagon. In the light of what happened in the prohibition years, not only in Chicago but in most of our major cities, it seems incredible that the town could then have been so free from armed assault.

Payrolls were not the only funds handled by Brink's, for 1900 saw the Company's first recorded transportation of bank funds. Six bags of silver dollars, each bag weighing 60 pounds, were moved from the Home National Bank at Halsted and Washington to the Federal Building. Sam Jones, one of Brink's "strong men" was in charge of the shipment. Jones made no effort at concealment. Upon reaching the Federal Building, he left the driver in charge of the buckboard, shouldered three bags of coins—180 pounds—carried them up three flights of stairs and down a long corridor to the receiving room. A second trip with a similar load and the job was done. It seems that Sam Jones took such a task lightly in more ways than one.

Old timers used to maintain that Brink's horses caused a good deal more excitement in these early days than did the threat of banditry. Each year a carload or two of mustangs from the ranges of the West were offered for sale at the Western Avenue yards on the basis of "take your pick for $25 a head." Small but wiry and tough, these half-broken horses were both cheap and well-suited to certain Brink's services. But, until well broken to harness, they frequently gave the drivers some exciting times. One of these mustang teams crashed through the swinging doors of a typical West Side saloon and was brought to a halt only by the rear wall. No one was actually hurt, but a surprising number of hoboes and Skid Row habitués brought in spurious personal injury claims.

Another famous animal was Charlie, a huge white with more energy than any horse ought to have and a mouth so tough that he was hard to control. To ease the strain on their aching arms, drivers made it a practice to pull in behind a horse car which would act as an automatic brake. On one occasion, Charlie set a record for wagon traffic by following a horse car through the tunnel under the Chicago River while the Brink's driver was delivering a payroll to the Cribben and Sexton plant.

Already in this period, Brink's had begun to expand. In 1903 it purchased Schneider's Chicago–Oak Park Express Co. for $2,750. Along with the business and good will went nine double and three single wagons, twelve horses and two mules. In February 1904, already having an office in Englewood, the directors voted to accept an offer for the construction and rental of a stable at 63rd Street and Cottage Grove, and a month later purchased the small express business of Wm. Daley & Co. in Evanston. Three new stations were thus in use.

Chicago had grown spectacularly. The census of 1900 credited the city with a population of barely under 1,700,000—and Brink's was growing along with it.

CHAPTER IV

Changing Times

THE TURN OF THE CENTURY was an exciting time, a time
of transition and change, of an accelerated tempo in business and social life. Already, on the streets of Chicago, a
fair number of the new horseless carriages or gas-buggies
were to be seen. Noisy and temperamental, subject to
frequent tire trouble and somewhat hazardous to crank,
they were primarily expensive toys ridiculed by the conservative, yelled at by small boys but accepted enthusi-
astically by the progressive and adventuresome.

Brink's, with its substantial investment in horses and
wagons, and with its emphasis upon dependable delivery
in any weather, would seem to be an unlikely candidate
for experimentation. Yet the Company was among the
leaders in testing the commercial application of the automobile. In November, 1904, the board of directors passed
the following motion:

The horse and wagon are like those used in earlier days. The 14 year old wagon boy is George Wons, still with Brink's after 46 years of service.

It frightened the horses, it was cursed by the drivers and hostlers who claimed that its fumes stank up the stables— and it demonstrated the progressive attitude of the Company. No one foresaw the immense scope of the revolution to be affected by the automobile, but Brink's at least indicated its adaptability and its awareness that this was a time of growth and progress, even though the horse was to remain the prime mover for nearly another decade.

Sometimes the signs of change are small. A brief note in the corporate minutes antedating the purchase of the Knox Gasoline Express Wagon marks another significant advance. Brink's drivers were given a new status and enlarged opportunity through the payment of commissions on pick-up and delivery business solicited by the men. Honesty and a strong back were no longer the sole criteria. The most successful drivers would also have to possess some of the attributes of a salesman.

There was another significant happening in 1904: the name of Dr. Frank Allen appeared for the first time in the minutes of the Company when he was commended by A. P. Brink for the excellent condition of the horses.

Frank Allen, after four years apprenticeship in a Liverpool bank, emigrated from England as a young man and came to New York. Here, as a medical student, it took only one experience in the operating room to convince him that surgery on human beings could never be his

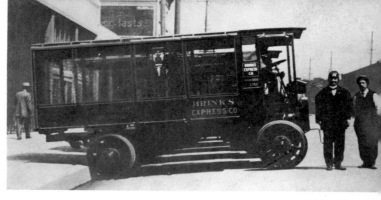

Hard-tired Autocar trucks like these are typical of express trucks used by Brink's before World War I.

field. He then turned to veterinary medicine and took his degrees from the American Veterinary College, New York, in March 1889.

Moving to St. Paul, Minnesota Dr. Allen was employed for several years in the management of the farm and racing stable owned by James J. Hill, the "Empire Builder" of railroad fame.

Late in the century, Dr. Allen and his family moved to Chicago where he took out an Illinois veterinarian's license and entered into practice. In a few years he was the attending veterinarian for a number of the large stables in the city, including that of Brink's.

In 1905, Frank Allen appears on the register as the owner of five shares of stock, a holding which he increased steadily over the years. In 1909, the Company's fiftieth year in business, he was named to the Board of Directors and a year later took his first title as Superintendent of Maintenance and Equipment. There is no record of a Golden Anniversary celebration.

Frank Allen's son, John D., had already been working for the Company since 1904 as was A. P. Brink's son Percy from an earlier date.

Meantime, there had been an interesting development. At the July directors meeting in 1907 it was moved to empower the General Manager and Secretary "to contract for the delivery *and distribution* of a weekly payroll"

for the Florsheim Shoe Company. The italics have been
added to point up the fact that this is the first recorded
instance in which Brink's made a written contract not only
to deliver a payroll but to place the funds in individual
pay envelopes and distribute them to employes. However, old timers clearly recall that such a service had
already been rendered to Hart, Schaffner & Marx for
several years.

This gradually evolved into the modern procedure
whereby a company, using any accepted business machine
method, prepares its pay envelopes and delivers them to
Brink's along with a check for the total payroll. Brink's
cashes the check, fills the individual pay envelopes, delivers them to the client's place of business and distributes
them to the employes, either from permanent armored
booths, from preselected guarded locations, or from mov-
able cashier's trays carried through office or plant.

To go back to the early nineteen hundreds, the Company had already purchased two additional "democrat
buggies" for money deliveries, and had authorized its
principal employes to sign for payroll funds at any
Chicago bank.

Moving money was on its way to becoming an important part of Brink's business. On January 1, 1913, Federal legislation increasing the scope of parcel post service
by authorizing the post office to handle much larger
packages, tolled a warning bell for all the express companies although it was more alarming to the inter-city
companies operating over the railroads than it was to
the local operators such as Brink's.

The major express companies were in very prosperous
circumstances. American Express Company was developing and expanding world-wide travel services including

Brink's Chicago City Express Co. wagon photographed in 1910. At left is Driver Munzenberger; right, Fred Woehrle.

the sale of money orders and travelers checks honored anywhere. In February 1910, Wells Fargo and Company declared its fabulous 300% dividend totalling $8 million in cash and $16 million in stock. Later in the same year, three additional 5% cash dividends were declared. The big companies were "fat cats" in the opinion of the press, and the public was ready for the new and lower priced parcel post.

By January 1, 1913 when parcel post service became effective, Brink's was doing as much money business as express business, and was earning practically all of its profits from the former source.

One last horse anecdote is worthy of mention. In June 1911, after Chicago's annual Work Horse Parade, Dr. Allen reported that Brink's horses won a silver cup valued at $100, three blue ribbons, four red ribbons and four yellow; also one gold, three silver and twenty-five bronze medals.

In 1911, Percy Brink quit his job to move west, and in 1912 was followed by A. P. Brink who resigned from the Company and went to California.

* * *

At this time operations of the Company were becoming increasingly motorized. Stables were being sold or leases allowed to lapse; barns were being converted to garages. The earliest express trucks were similar to the Autocars illustrated on page 41—very modern, at least in the respect that they were cab-over-engine design. Not so modern in the side cranks, hard tires and gas lamps. Payrolls and other moneys were being moved in standard touring cars usually with a small safe fitted in the tonneau.

Following Woodrow Wilson's election in 1912 business slowed down, and the outbreak of World War I in August 1914, put a further damper on the economy. To allay the general concern about the effects of the great conflict, the administration coined the phrase, "Business as usual." However, before the war had continued for long, the Allies turned to the United States for munitions and supplies. These added demands were soon taxing the production of factories and farms.

Brink's was also expanding in order to meet new calls on its services. When the United States entered the war on April 17, 1917, Dr. Allen had become General Manager of Brink's and J. D. Allen was on the board of directors. Naturally, the Company suffered the loss of many young and able crew men who volunteered or were drafted into service.

A special Banking Department was formed with offices in the First National Bank Building and J. D. Allen was named as its manager. In spite of war conditions the Company, during the year 1918, opened its first branch office in Cleveland, Ohio solely to handle money and valuables. The Money Movers were hitting their stride.

As a war measure in 1918, the Federal government,

This 1921 banquet photo shows, clockwise from top: Dr. Frank Allen, Mr. F. A. McAllister, Frank Holland, William Turney, Walter Hampton, William English, J. D. Allen, Ed Whitted, O. K. Simms, Roy Meader, J. Raichart, C. S. Swan, William Obenshein and B. A. Kennedy.

acting through the Railroad Administration, took over Adams, American, Southern and Wells Fargo express companies. Their operations were consolidated under the American Railway Express Company. The consolidation never was dissolved. Eventually, the American Railway Express Company was succeeded by the Railway Express Agency, owned by 86 railroads, which purchased the equipment and express business of the four companies. Excluded from the business for which they were organized, it is a tribute to the resourcefulness of the express companies that they were able to carry on successfully in other pursuits. The misfortunes of the express companies which followed government seizure of the railroads are only one example of the many ills resulting from this socialistic experiment.

J. H. Bradley, President of Brink's since 1886 and one of the original incorporators, was living in the East and attending only one or two Board meetings a year. Mr. Bradley's long career with the American Express Company had carried him from Traffic Manager in Chicago to the home office in New York where he became Gen-

45

eral Traffic Manager, then Vice President and a director. He had expressed himself as being opposed to any expansion by Brink's. He was displeased by the opening of the Cleveland office and, when the Banking Department proposed opening in Rochester, N. Y., Bradley came to Chicago.

After a conference with Brink's officers, he accepted an offer to buy his stock tendered by Dr. Allen, J. D. Allen and W. B. Wyne. As soon as the deal was consummated, he resigned as President of the Company and his son Ralph resigned as Secretary. Dr. Allen succeeded as President, and William English, the Company's legal advisor, became Secretary.

During 1919, the surprising fact was revealed that Brink's charter had never been recorded in the Recorder's Office of Cook County as then required by law. The Company had therefore been a *de facto* corporation for forty years. This is no more than an interesting sidelight as there were no untoward results, but it was necessary to reincorporate the Company to correct the situation.

With offices in Cleveland and Rochester, Brink's, during the month of January 1920, dropped "Chicago City" from its name and became simply, Brink's Express Company handling almost entirely money and valuables.

The post-war years were the end of an era for Brink's, the end of an era for the United States. The country was deeply affected by the new internationalism, the expansion of foreign trade, stepped-up industrialization, even by the gang warfare that had its roots in the national resistance to prohibition. The thought expressed at the opening of this chapter can be repeated: it was a time of ferment and of change, a time in which Brink's speedily adapted itself to the new conditions

CHAPTER V

Expansion in U.S. and Canada

MANY MIDDLE-AGED and older people are inclined to look back somewhat nostalgically to the "gay twenties." Without rose colored glasses, it may not have been especially gay, but it was certainly an exciting time. With only minor setbacks, our economy was cresting up to the giant wave that would break and fall with such an earth-shattering roar on October 29, 1929.

It was an exciting time for Brink's because it was a period of rapid growth. The Company was now under the control of Dr. Frank Allen and his son, John D., with W. B. Wyne still an influential factor in the corporation

The following account of the opening of the first branches is put down here as it was told by John D. Allen and others, or drawn from available records.

The two Allens did not always see eye to eye, yet they complemented each other admirably and formed an excellent management team. The father was conservative, a shrewd money manager with a sharp eye for the details of corporate and financial affairs. The son was a dynamic salesman with the deep conviction that money moving was destined to become a necessary integral part

Armored car and open convoy at Worcester, Massachusetts, Branch in 1924.

of banking and business. Brink's had pioneered in the field and J. D. was determined to make it the unchallenged leader.

Like other chronicles of growth and achievement, the whole effort seems simple in the telling—but it is rarely so in the forward progress of a business.

The virgin soil was tough and unyielding, the spade work difficult. But J. D. Allen persisted with assistance from Kenneth C. Allen, then assistant superintendent, and from other Company associates. (*"K.C." now Vice President in charge of business development, is not related to the Frank Allen family. He came up from an armored car crew as have many other officials and practically all supervisors and branch managers of Brink's, Incorporated.*)

In Brink's case, opening a new branch also meant launching a specialized transportation service entirely new to the community that was entered. After the potentialities of the market had been surveyed, suitable, centrally located quarters lending themselves to the proper security measures had to be selected, adequate vaults installed and the necessary equipment procured.

Thereafter the job became two-fold. On the one hand, carefully screening and training the necessary personnel under time-tested Brink's rules. On the other, selling

Brink's services tailored to suit local banking and business practices.

With no armored service in the community, prospects had to be educated from scratch on its advantages. Long established habits had to be changed. A firm accustomed to having its payrolls and bank deposits carried through the streets by a trusted employe had to be convinced that it was exposing that employe to injury or death as well as risking the loss of the cash he carried. It also had to be shown that Brink's service was actually less costly than having deposits made by an owner or his employe, and was therefore an economy rather than an added expense.

Another obstacle to be overcome lay in the fact that, in some cities, uniformed police escorts were reluctantly supplied by the Police Department free or at a nominal charge (a situation that still exists in some communities). This was fine for the merchants using the service but manifestly unfair to the taxpayers. Civic officials had to be convinced that police manpower could and should be used only for work benefiting the entire community.

Once having gained a foothold, Brink's had to consolidate its position by providing services so useful and efficient that they were quickly recognized as necessary and valuable adjuncts to banking and business.

Franchises to operate usually had to be cleared with the police as well as with other local governmental departments concerned with public safety. After all, Brink's operation required the parking of armored cars on busy thoroughfares and the presence of men with guns drawn on sidewalks, in streets and in banks and office buildings. Nevertheless, many farsighted officials, civic leaders and law enforcement officers welcomed the

Money Movers service seeing in it a useful deterrent to crime. Brink's men released for regular patrol duty the many policemen formerly assigned to guarding money on the move. The armored cars and armed guards discouraged attempts at holdups that all too often had resulted in shootings on busy streets. In fact, Chicago police records demonstrated that street assaults on payrolls and bank deposits were virtually eliminated when handled by Brink's.

Right from the start it was Brink's policy never to sacrifice dependability of service or security of cargo or personnel for the sake of false economy. No changes were made to meet cutthroat competition in the required number of men in a crew or amount of insurance carried.

As experience was gained, the establishment of branches was governed by a highly competent, on-the-spot appraisal of whether a community could reasonably be expected to support a Brink's branch office.

Brink's first branch was opened in Cleveland, Ohio in July, 1918 in response to a suggestion by one of Cleveland's larger banks that the service was needed. Late in 1919 several Rochester, N. Y. clothing manufacturing companies petitioned the Company to open a branch office in their city to handle their payrolls, and this was done on January 1, 1920. Next was an important move—a branch was opened in New York City on January 2, 1922.

In the Fall of 1920, the Philadelphia Bank Association invited Brink's to submit a plan providing armored car service in the city. Pennsylvania laws permitted branch banking. This meant that the larger banks in Philadelphia each had numerous small branches that were little more than service offices and lacked vaults for the safekeeping of funds. Each day at the close of banking hours,

First Brink's armored car and crew in Erie, Pa., 1927. Crewmen are wearing earliest style uniforms with puttees and Sam Browne belts.

the main bank collected all the currency for overnight storage and re-distributed it to the branches on the following morning. A truck breakdown meant a late opening for the affected branches, and impaired service.

The invitation to Brink's included a guarantee that the banks participating would discontinue using their own vehicles. Following protracted negotiations an agreement was concluded. Brink's was thereafter licensed by the State of Pennsylvania and the new Philadelphia branch was opened on January 13, 1922.

The establishment of Brink's service in Philadelphia and the elimination of the individual truck fleets by the participating banks proved highly successful. The banks made annual savings of many thousands of dollars, and greatly improved the service to their branches.

Philadelphia was the largest bank operation to that date for Brink's and it helped to pave the way for what has become an exceedingly important phase of the business in all branches. It was in the early days in Philadelphia that Otto D. Plank, now Vice President—Opera-

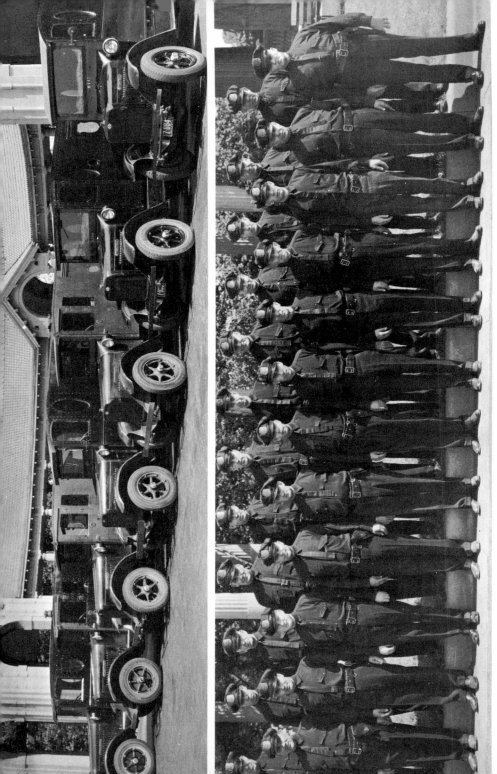

These seven armored cars were the entire fleet at Kansas City Branch in 1929.

Crewmen pictured the same day in later type, police style uniforms. Uniform styles have changed periodically.

tions, joined the Branch as a driver. Working up rapidly through the ranks to the position of Eastern Director of Operations in charge of about 35 branches, Mr. Plank played a large part in developing Brink's present system of operations.

Every banking day Brink's moves millions of dollars in currency, coin, securities, and other valuables for large banks, their branches and correspondent banks, and for the Federal Reserve Banks and branches. It also moves regular and registered mail and express between post offices, airports, express offices and the banks. In many cities Brink's handles a huge volume of bank clearings between the Clearing House, correspondent banks and individual banks. These services simplify the transportation problem of banks, protect them against the loss of property in transit, eliminate the hazards of injury to bank messengers from armed holdup, and create good will for the banks with their depositors.

With Cleveland, Rochester, New York and Philadelphia opened, Brink's drive to achieve status as a national money-moving organization was well under way.

In 1923, Brink's opened Branches in Detroit, Newark, and Providence; in 1924 Pittsburgh, Worcester, Syracuse, St. Louis, Kansas City and Minneapolis; in 1925 Toledo, Boston and Buffalo. In all, between 1922 and 1932, forty-nine Branches were established in cities as

A Brink's armored car at the Fourth National Bank, Wichita, Kansas in 1931. Banks were already becoming important customers.

ROGER
COMPLETE FOOD MARKET

Making a pick up at a Cincinnati chain store in 1932. Chain organizations were an important factor in Brink's expansion at this period.

far apart as Portland, Maine and Los Angeles, California.

In many cases, contracts with chain store organizations, such as The Great Atlantic & Pacific Tea Company and The Kroger Co., were important aids in the establishment of new offices because of their many locations which afforded a community-wide base upon which to expand. Such national accounts have been and still are major factors in the extension of Brink's operations.

Brink's attained international stature in 1927 when Brink's Express Company of Canada, Limited was organized. Branches were opened in Montreal and Toronto.

Expansion on this scale during the twenties naturally involved many problems, especially since it was accompanied by a change in corporate policy which had eliminated extension of the express side of the business. In fact, the branches never handled anything but money and valuables.

The articles of incorporation of Brink's were amended in 1923 so that the corporate powers would enable it to engage legally in the extensive services offered as a national organization.

The rapid growth of the Money Movers was slowed down in the early '30s by a depression that, for depth and duration, has not been equaled in modern times.

CHAPTER VI

Some Dramatic Events

THE HISTORIC stock market crash of late 1929 was promptly followed by a business depression which touched bottom in the early '30s and rapidly became world-wide in scope. Prices dropped steadily and swiftly; corporate securities sold at mere fractions of their former values with few takers; commercial paper and real estate values sagged; unemployment rose to record levels with many of those still employed working only part time or at reduced pay. It was a period of bread lines, of apple sellers, the P.W.A., the W.P.A., the N.R.A. and of "brother, can you spare a dime."

Just as the boom period had been founded on false optimism, so the depression was based, at least in part, on pessimism and fear.

Among the chief sufferers were America's banks. Some of them were in real difficulties simply because loans, which had seemed well secured by adequate collateral, were on dangerous ground. Many banks found their liquid assets seriously depleted. Other banks, still in good financial condition, were almost equally endangered by the threat of "runs" that often developed within hours on no more foundation than whispered rumor or gossip.

Most frequently, runs developed at neighborhood, suburban and country banks when checking and savings account depositors queued up in panic to withdraw their funds. On a good many occasions, such runs were broken merely by the appearance of a Brink's armored car bringing additional cash from a larger bank or from the Federal Reserve Bank or branches.

If panic grows on fear and rumor, it withers in the face of common sense and confidence. Very often the lines of frightened depositors melted rapidly away at this tangible evidence of solvency. Sometimes it was only a matter of hours before the early withdrawals were flowing back into the bank. It has often been stated that the timely appearance of a Brink's armored car had all the drama associated with the arrival of the U. S. Cavalry at a beleaguered outpost in the early days of the West.

The Moratorium

As early as the evening of February 12, 1933 the Manager of Brink's Detroit Branch was aware that something unusual was afoot. He was called to a mysterious meeting of the officers of the First National Bank and told to have two armored cars with five-man crews at the bank at seven sharp the following morning.

This was so unusual that he promptly called the Home Office in Chicago to tell them the story and seek more information. Within hours he received the electrifying news from Chicago that all Detroit banks would close the next day, that an armored car load of small silver for change had been ordered to be sent from Brink's Cleveland Branch and that he should stand by for trouble.

Imagine the situation of a big city without a bank!

Remember the bank moratorium? It was more than three days in many places. Reproduced from a bound copy of the *Chicago Daily Tribune*.

If the normal flow of cash ceases and it simply accumulates in the hands of sellers, business dries up in a matter of days and immense hardships result.

Brink's acted swiftly. Additional armored cars were ordered in from Chicago, Cleveland and Toledo. As quickly as possible 80 new men were hired and put to work with the barest instructions. Shifts of men kept the armored cars on the move; the office force worked twenty hours a day. Half a million dollars were moved every day to Saginaw and Bay City alone. Service also was provided to Flint, Lansing and other communities.

Rapidly the crisis spread to other branches across the nation. On Saturday, March 4, 1933, newspaper headlines announced that the President had declared a nationwide bank holiday to begin on Monday. After the government auditors had made their examinations, banks in sound financial condition were to be re-opened.

In Chicago many customers, unable to make normal bank deposits, were sending in funds to be held for them in Brink's vaults. Hundreds of other businesses, not customers of Brink's, were phoning for help.

On Sunday morning Brink's decided to rent the currently unoccupied space in a new building on LaSalle and Monroe Streets in Chicago that had been designed to accommodate a bank. Phone lines were run in and the necessary equipment to carry on delivery operations was installed. Scores of clerks were hired to sort and count the money, and keep the records.

K. C. Allen, then superintendent, was moved into the new quarters. J. D. Allen shuttled back and forth between the "bank" offices and the Home Office then at 571 West Jackson Boulevard. It is said that these two, along with Dr. Frank Allen, organized one of the most complex and successful "banking" operations in history.

Many organizations such as chain stores, transportation systems and national oil companies, had more coin and currency than they could use or safely store. Others urgently needed money for payrolls, change and other purposes. In fact, the need for meeting payrolls throughout the country was of paramount importance.

Brink's, in effect, played the part of a giant national bank. With the full permission of its depositors, it took in, paid out and transferred funds. In many cases, company receipts were checked and sorted by Brink's, made into necessary payrolls and the balance retained or loaned for use by other companies.

One executive walked into the LaSalle Street office and tossed on a desk an envelope containing a hundred and fifty $1000 bills along with a list of addresses where he wanted them delivered. By the latter part of the week Brink's was handling some 800 daily express shipments of funds in addition to its other duties.

All of this was unprecedented. Bank officials visited the new office to check on how things were being handled and expressed their confidence that Brink's was equal to the emergency. At the week's end, the Chicago vaults alone held some 40,000 deposits, with $45,000,000 in cash waiting to go back into the banks when they re-opened.

Through all of the crisis, Brink's went busily but methodically about its job of sorting, counting, checking, transferring and moving money, keeping the wheels of commerce and business going, bringing some sort of order and normality to a wildly disordered situation. Much of the work was done by untrained forces supervised by a nucleus of veteran employees. When it was over, to the astonishment of bankers not a penny had been lost. The Money Movers had again demonstrated the qualities of integrity, resourcefulness and accuracy on which their success had been built. Business had turned to Brink's for help in this time of crisis—and Brink's had come through.

It is interesting to note that the tremendous volume of work done through the moratorium brought Brink's little or no profit. But, according to a public statement made by Frank Allen at that time, it was not a profit venture, being undertaken primarily as a public service. There were no set rates for these special services. All paid something. Some concerns voluntarily paid generous sums. If thought excessive, refunds were made by Brink's.

Moving Bank and Insurance Company Assets

Periodically, though certainly not often enough to become a routine matter, a bank or a large insurance company calls upon the Money Movers to transfer its assets to a new location. When the bank is a really big one, it can well be imagined that the logistical problems assume something of the complexities of D-Day.

Let's take, as an example, the move made for a large bank in Philadelphia.

It could not legally suspend its operations. The inconvenience to its customers and the general disruption of its

A 1935 bank move in Sharon, Pennsylvania. Gray armored car in the background is one of the first aluminum bodies. The Guard alongside the bank building is W. L. Cole, now Safety Director of Security and Protection Department.

business made this impractical. Therefore, it had to make its move sometime between the close of banking on Friday or Saturday and the re-opening Monday morning. By that time, all records and accounts had to be in order and the staff ready to do business as usual.

This alone was a colossal job. Add to it the fact that there were in excess of six hundred millions of assets consisting of cash, stocks, bonds and valuable papers that had to be moved and it became an operation to haunt the dreams of bank personnel.

Do you think that was too much money to tempt a hold-up gang? That no one would dare stage an assault? Then ask yourself whether you would chance the risk of an unguarded move. Of course, you wouldn't! Only the certain fore-knowledge of iron-clad security measures will deter armed assault on such a treasure.

With the transfer set for 8:00 a.m., seven Brink's armored cars manned by a total of 35 formidably armed men and supervisory personnel pulled up to the bank. Other Brink's armored cars and armed crews of five men each stationed at intersections along the route provided strong points, and also were available should one of the transporting armored cars break down. City police were

A typical modern day bank move. Photo made in 1957 when Philadelphia's Provident Trust Co. and Tradesmen's Bank & Trust Co. merged to form the Provident Tradesmen's Bank & Trust Co., fourth largest bank in the city.

detailed to guard the streets at both the old and the new premises, and radio-equipped police cruisers patrolled the route.

Methodically, the Brink's men signed for sealed containers of currency and sealed files containing securities and other valuable documents, loaded them into armored cars and were dispatched according to a schedule arranged so that they would arrive at the new location and be immediately unloaded. The amount transported on each armored car was limited to 30 million dollars. In nine and one-half hours the transfer was completed. Not a penny was lost, not even any real excitement except for the moment when a bemused "skid row" denizen tried to stop two Brink's men on the sidewalk to cadge a dime for a cup of coffee. The poor fellow probably doesn't know to this day why the police hustled him against the wall so swiftly and frisked him for a weapon.

Each year Brink's makes a number of such bank and insurance company transfers. Planned and timed down to the smallest detail they are executed with a precision that would be the envy of a crack division launching an attack. There is no advance publicity, no whirring of newsreel cameras. Yet secrecy is impossible. Hundreds,

(Above) Brink's transported England's historic Magna Carta from the Cunard dock in New York to the Jamestown, Va. Festival where it was exhibited in April 1957.

(Left) Brink's served Chicago's "Century of Progress" in 1933. The armored car is in front of the "English Village" exhibit.

(Left, below) Guarding more than a million silver dollars at a trade show. The occasion is described on the opposite page.

(Below) Bill Leyden, master of ceremonies of the TV quiz show "It Could Be You" exhibits currency guarded by Brink's.

even thousands of people must know the approximate time the move will take place. Normal vehicular and pedestrian traffic is usually undisturbed.

Money . . . Historic Documents . . . Art Objects . . . Jewels . . . Unusual Items

It would be easy to compile a long and astonishing list of valuables moved and guarded by Brink's for special events or occasions—and an even more astonishing one of the requests made by companies or individuals who simply wanted to cash in on the publicity value of one of the gray and blue armored cars with its smartly uniformed crew.

Some of our readers may have seen Brink's men on national television shows such as "You Asked For It" when the request was made to show a million dollars in cash. That "million" is a magic figure with tremendous popular appeal and many such displays have been made.

In April 1955, three Brink's tractor-trailers hauled thirty-six tons of silver dollars—1,209,467 of them—from the Treasury in Washington, D.C. to a convention hall in Cleveland. There the huge hoard of silver was spread on the floor of the booth of the Gold Seal Company, makers of Glass Wax, for display during the Super Market Institute convention. Brink's guards remained on duty through the show. They reported that the silver would "flow" through the night giving off a faint but almost constant jingle. As the coins were unused, they retained a certain amount of silver dust. When re-bagging them at the end of the exhibition, this dust rose in a silver haze about four feet in the air. It caused a sickeningly sweet taste and finally became so bad that the Brink's men were forced to mask their noses and mouths with handker-

Ten Brink's armored cars moved valuables of many kinds from the mansion of Colonel Edward H. R. Green. In charge of the move was the man at the extreme left—Otto Plank, now Vice President–Operations.

chiefs. After the recount of the coins by the Treasury in Washington, it was found that only 17 were missing although thousands of people had handled and even walked over the money.

When Colonel Edward H. R. Green, son of the famous and eccentric financier Hetty Green, died in 1936, his big granite home in Dartmouth, Mass., about 75 miles from Boston, was filled with valuables. A convoy of ten Brink's armored cars with a police escort loaded $20,-000,000 worth of jewelry and precious stones, stamp, currency and coin collections, and various art objects, and transported them to the First National Bank of Boston for safekeeping. It was perhaps the largest move ever made of private property.

Brink's has also transported and guarded the "Crown of the Andes" which was made by the Inca Indians of Peru many centuries ago. Carved from solid gold and heavily encrusted with emeralds, the crown has great intrinsic worth to which is added its value as an antiquity.

Value of an entirely different sort was represented by

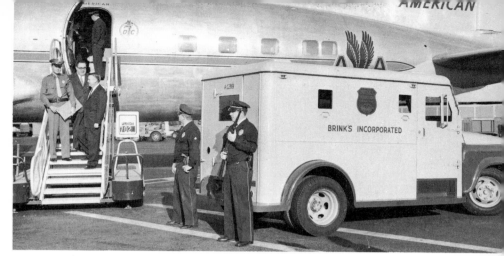

Original of "Gettysburg Address" being entrusted to Brink's at Los Angeles.

the Magna Carta (see picture on page 62) and the original manuscript of Lincoln's Gettysburg Address handled in a move pictured above.

Things Brink's has been requested to transport range from millions in phony money to a plaster cast of a movie star's legs (the flesh and blood ones reputedly insured for five million dollars); new models and new products to be shown at trade fairs; prizes of all sorts. In general, Brink's agrees to cooperate only when the object has a reasonably high intrinsic or historical value, and when it is to be paid for at an agreed rate and handled in a business-like fashion without horseplay.

Among special money moves—at least in the sense that they are not regularly scheduled on a day in and day out basis—are those made in connection with sports events, expositions, fairs and large charity fund raising drives.

Among the hundreds of such events served by the Money Movers are the Canadian National Exhibition at Toronto, Ontario; Chicago Tribune Charities All Star football game, Golden Gloves and Music Festival; the Army-Navy football game, the Rose Bowl football game and the Kentucky Derby.

CHAPTER VII

Cars...Crews...Safes...Insurance

THE READER WILL RECALL that Brink's first money deliveries were made with a horse and buggy. As the automobile gained reliability, standard open touring cars carried the money and the armed guards. Following the first payroll robbery in Brink's history, which occurred in 1917, additional security was sought by having this vehicle trailed by a "convoy car"—usually a Ford Model "T" carrying a driver and another guard.

By the end of World War I, the so-called "school bus" design was in use with steel bars protecting the windows. Again, convoy cars were used and the first tentative experiments with armor were made.

When bullet-proof safety glass in thicknesses of three-quarters of an inch and up appeared on the market, the development of armor was begun in earnest. Brink's first car with a fully armored body went into service in 1923. Boiler plate steel of fairly light gauge was used because the low-powered vehicles of the day quickly lost maneuverability with serious increases in weight.

It was not until after the 1927 dynamiting, detailed in Chapter VIII, that the first fully armored cars as known

66

This is one of the "school bus" money trucks used by Brink's about 1920. Model "T" behind it is a convoy car.

Armored coupes like this were bought as late as 1940.

today made their appearance. They were still cumbersome, still lacking in many modern refinements, but body designs improved steadily keeping pace with engine and chassis developments.

By the early thirties, specially hardened aluminum was being used as armor and, along with the light, surface hardened steels now available, is still enjoying wide use.

Power driven ventilating systems with roof intakes have made the cars more comfortable and have removed the fear of successful gas attack. Firing ports are so placed around the car that there are no blind spots from which an attacker can shoot in safety, and bullet-proof glass has become as resistant as the armor itself.

In addition to the handguns carried by crew members, armored cars on certain occasions are provided with an arsenal of shotguns, high powered rifles and tear gas weapons. There is a money chest in which funds are stored so that they are safely guarded even in the event of a highway accident of such severity that it breaks open the vehicle's doors and disables the crew. An armored bulkhead separates the driver's cab and rear compartment. There is a special switch in the latter which permits cutting the engine ignition should robbers overpower the driver, and another which sounds a siren alarm to summon aid.

Drivers are so carefully schooled in "defensive driving"

These six armored cars constituted the Buffalo, N. Y., fleet in 1928.

One of the larger size armored cars currently in use is pictured here in front of Brink's Chicago office. This type is frequently used in Federal Reserve Bank service.

that they have established some remarkable safety records for these heavy vehicles. Skilled mechanics keep them in topnotch condition so that breakdowns and delays are extremely rare.

Charles W. Allen, Senior Vice President of Brink's, is in charge of the construction and responsible for the performance of the armored car fleet. Today's models, developed by Mr. Allen with the cooperation of custom body builders, can be said to be as nearly impregnable to attack as it is possible to make a vehicle designed to operate not only on city streets, but to keep up with highway traffic on over-the-road runs. Because of its pioneering efforts Brink's can justly claim the leading role in the development of the armored car.

Armored car costs vary from about $7500 for an average-size car to $25,000 for an armored semi-trailer such as is used in transporting coin for the United States Mint and in other special services. Since 1940 Brink's armored cars have been painted battleship gray with dark blue striping. The Brink's shield in blue, gold and red, appears on each side of the armored car and on the rear door if design permits.

Over the years, steady progress has been made in methods of selecting personnel, in developing the "book of rules" governing crew procedures, and in the training of crews. Security was the watchword every step of the way.

Trained personnel and equipment were the two vital elements not only in preventing successful attack, but in discouraging any attack at all. They are elements which have made Brink's name synonymous in the public mind with safety in transit and delivery.

Select Personnel

Brink's personnel, especially those applying for positions as crewmen or in money rooms where large sums must be skillfully counted, are selected with the utmost care. Each applicant must provide a detailed chronological record of his activities from birth and must agree to a rigorous investigation of his background. This is first carried out by the Company itself through the normal channels of references, credit ratings and police records; then, in a more intensive fashion, by an investigative agency employed by Brink's and supervised by the insurance underwriters. Standards are strict, yet no candidate is rejected merely on suspicion. When some slight doubt exists, Brink's frequently spends considerable additional sums on a lengthy detailed investigation to be sure that it is not unfairly rejecting a qualified applicant.

It is a system that has worked well over the years. So well that petty peculations have been extremely rare and attempts at substantial thefts could be ticked off on the fingers of one hand.

It is interesting to note that most Brink's men are veterans of the armed forces; many have had police training.

Biggest armored vehicle is this truck-trailer combination put in service in 1958.

Driver Carl Anderson gets award for 25 years of safe driving. From left: Gordon Hall, Assistant Vice President—Operations; William Harvey, Manager, Chicago Branch; Parker T. Jones, Sr., Treasurer; Eugene E. Murphy, President; Driver Anderson; Charles W. Allen, Sr., Vice President.

Basically, Brink's men must be endowed with good character and strong physique. They must be honest, courageous and courteous. They like their jobs and, as they become seasoned, develop a high degree of efficiency along with a wary cautiousness in keeping with their responsibilities. Their fidelity to the Brink's corps is demonstrated by their performance throughout the years.

What prompts a man to seek a job with Brink's? Don Hoagland, Assistant Vice President—Business Development, who served as a guard, driver and messenger, said:

"A man likes a job on a Brink's armored car because it's clean work, not like ordinary trucking. You never have to handle any objectionable cargo. While you can't have a weak back and still handle bags of coin, neither do you wrestle any really heavy loads. Job security is another important consideration. Brink's men are not subject to lay-offs at every economic ripple. Here are some other pluses. Each day in an armored car is just a little different—you never know what's around the corner. The routine changes and there's a touch of adventure. Because of your uniform, you are always respected and received cordially. I met many nice people when making route 'stops'—customers who became good friends. Hours are a favorable factor, too. You turn in your gun and get out of uniform after the day's run and are as free as the air."

What is the most difficult situation that Brink's men

ordinarily have to face? That's easy—it's the teen-age or adult comic who, hand in coat pocket, steps up behind a guard and mutters "This is a stick-up." It is a tribute to the steadiness and reliability of Brink's men that none of these jokers has yet been shot.

The Armored Car Crew

Many readers may be interested in the make-up and functioning of the crew of an armored car. It is headed by a Messenger who is responsible for all shipments and is in command of the vehicle and its crew. As the contact between the customer's representative and Brink's, the Messenger is also responsible for collecting the sealed shipments and must obtain a signed receipt for each one delivered to a cashier at Brink's office or to a bank teller or other consignee. Second in rank among the crew is the Driver. Finally, there are one, two or more Guards depending upon the value of the shipments to be handled by a given armored crew. Incidentally, three-fourths of Brink's employes are members of armored car crews.

Each man is trained in small arms markmanship, must fire regularly on a range and must pass periodic qualifying tests. Many of them are enthusiasts who compete on Brink's own pistol teams or belong to gun clubs in their localities and often compete in national competition. The average robber reckless enough to chance "shooting it out" is likely to find the odds stacked against him.

The standard weapon is a .38 caliber revolver. It is supplied by Brink's and always worn by the individual on

Brink's crewmen practice regularly on the target range to maintain pistol proficiency. This man is firing at a target simulating a human torso.

Crewmen remain properly dispersed. One Guard is in the back of the armored car as the Messenger approaches; another Guard has remained on the sidewalk to cover the Messenger from the rear.

duty and is carried in the hand while money is being transported in the open.

Every crewman must know the security rules thoroughly and agrees that he may be dismissed instantly if he fails to comply with them. These rules are explicit and detailed concerning every phase of normal operation. They state the order in which men shall leave the car, who shall remain in it, the position and spacing of men while moving between the car and the point of pick-up or deposit, who shall handle and sign for shipments, procedures for re-entering the car and numerous other items all designed to assure safe operation with a minimum of risk to the public, the armored car crew and the shipment.

As an additional security measure, dispatchers at irregular intervals change the routing and scheduling of armored cars under their supervision. This makes it more difficult for potential hold-up men to plan their operations on a time schedule correlated to that of the Brink's crew.

The firearms used by Brink's employees are cared for by men qualified as armorers who check the weapons frequently for functioning and condition. They are regularly oiled, serviced and tested, and ammunition is replaced at frequent intervals so that there can be no malfunctioning or failure to fire in an emergency.

Brink's Pick-Up and Deposit Service, and Two-Key Safes

Brink's pick-up, deposit and change service provides a method of handling funds which relieves the merchant and his employes of the risk of injury or death and the loss of funds from holdup while transporting deposits to the bank or returning with change. Deposits collected after banking hours and on bank holidays are placed in Brink's vaults and deposited on the next banking day, thus making it unnecessary for customers to carry over large sums on their premises with the attendant risks.

To supplement its pick-up and deposit service, Brink's in 1927 introduced its "Cash Protector" types of two-key safes intended to protect up to $1000. Six years later the line was extended with a heavier series of safes for larger amounts of money. Brink's safes have gained recognition as the surest means of safeguarding accumulated funds and protecting employes in business establishments. Many authorities consider them far superior to the strongest combination-lock safes.

The combination lock has a fatal flaw. Someone must know the combination and can be forced to reveal it. He can be kidnapped from his home at night and made to open the safe while his family is held as hostages.

Brink's Two-Key Safes and Cash Protectors obviate this danger. The Cash Protector has a single compartment with a two-key door. Funds are simply dropped through a pick-proof slot. The Safes have two separate compartments. The outer compartment is intended for the storage of a nominal amount of currency and coin to be used for making change. It is protected by a burglar proof door locked by a combination lock, and the combination is known only to the customer. Behind the outer door is an inner compartment into which envelopes containing accumulated currency and checks are frequently deposited through a pick-proof slot in the inner compartment wall. The inner compartment door is locked by a two-key safety deposit box type lock.

The customer is furnished one key and Brink's messenger carries the guard key. Both keys must be operated simultaneously to open the inner compartment door. Brink's messenger guards the customer while individual envelopes are being removed from the inner compartment and made into a sealed deposit, which the messenger receipts for and delivers to bank or other consignee.

The safe user *cannot* open the inner compartment and *hold-up men know that he cannot!* A large sign in the office or store and a sign on the safe make this fact clear. Furthermore, the robber can try the customer's key for himself.

This fact is so widely known among criminals that it has greatly reduced the number of kidnapings for purposes of robbery. Indeed, many a merchant has attempted to buy or rent a Brink's sign knowing that it would of itself dis-

Three safe signs tell the same story in different ways.

This model is typical of larger Brink's safes designed to protect sums up to $25,000.

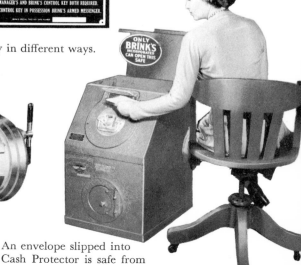

An envelope slipped into Cash Protector is safe from robbery, covered by insurance.

courage attempted holdups. A Brink's safe not only brings a feeling of security, but makes it unnecessary to carry expensive holdup and kidnapping insurance protection on the funds contained in the inner compartment.

Brink's Two-Key Safes are built to the Company's own registered designs by The Mosler Safe Co. Since their introduction, specifications have been revised from time to time. New models have been built and carefully tested to combat the latest methods of attack by burglars, and to incorporate the newest available torch and drill resistant materials and locking devices. They are tested by Underwriters Laboratories, Inc. and are classified as entitled to the lowest burglary insurance rates. They are never sold or rented but are provided only as a part of Brink's service.

Development of All Risk Insurance

As moving money and valuables grew in importance in Brink's business, and as the number of branches increased, it became necessary to provide for more complete insurance protection against all risks of loss or damage from any cause whatsoever to money, securities and valuables entrusted to the Company. What was needed was a single comprehensive policy that would replace the numerous policies and fidelity bonds hitherto in effect.

In 1926 H. Edward Reeves, then a Vice President of Joyce & Company, insurance brokers, and later President of Brink's, interested the Commercial Union Assurance Company of London, England, one of the world's largest marine insurance underwriters, in designing a single policy to insure all of the risks inherent in the transportation of money, securities and other valuables by armored car as is done for ships and their cargoes.

Just three days after the Coverdale robbery, the Commercial Union Assurance Co. Ltd. made good the loss to Brink's with this check for the full amount.

The following year the first such policy ever issued to an armored car company was issued to Brink's in the amount of two and one-half million dollars. As new forms of service were inaugurated and greater values were transported, the policy has been revised to include such services in its protection, and has been increased to fifteen million dollars on each armored car, each office and each place where liability is assumed. On January 1, 1959, the Commercial Union Assurance Company, Limited issued its 32nd consecutive renewal of Brink's all risk insurance policy. War risks, no longer insurable except on the high seas, are the only risks not covered.

It is an interesting sidelight that the Coverdale robbery, described in Chapter VIII, took place within 90 days after the first policy was issued. Almost $104,000 was stolen and a check for the amount was immediately given to Brink's by the insurance company. Though $38,000 was recovered and returned to the underwriters, their ultimate loss of about $66,000 was more than the amount of the first annual premium. The following year the insurance company renewed the policy without question.

It has been demonstrated on many occasions that it takes only a phone call and about ten minutes time for Brink's to acquire many millions of dollars of additional insurance for an emergency or a special money move of unusual size. This probably could not be said of any other organization in the United States.

CHAPTER VIII

Men with Guns

. . . the Story of Banditry in Modern Times

ON THE AFTERNOON of August 28, 1917 the roar of shot-guns on Chicago's west side broke a 26-year quiet in which no Brink's employe had been attacked while delivering money. It was the first sign that the organized banditry of the old West had appeared in a metropolitan setting.

On this hot afternoon three armed Brink's men had picked up a $9100 payroll at the Corn Exchange National Bank and driven to Winslow Bros., ornamental iron and brass manufacturers, at 4600 Harrison St. When they arrived a large maroon touring car, driver at the wheel and engine idling, was parked across the street from the plant.

Messenger Barton Allen, a son of Dr. Frank Allen, got out of the Brink's vehicle with a satchel of money in either hand and started up the walk. As he approached a clump of evergreen shrubbery, a shotgun roared and a charge of buckshot crashed into his head killing him instantly.

Four bandits leaped from the bushes. One seized the money bags. Another forced Guard Lewis from the Brink's car and disarmed him. Driver Osenberg, attempting to draw his revolver, was riddled with slugs. In less than a minute the bandits had gained their car and made their escape.

The Police Department reacted swiftly and effectively. On a tip from a jealous woman, one of the bandits named Carrao was picked up and he quickly implicated Wheed, Asciutto and Therien. On August 30th Wheed, known variously as "Blackie" and "Ammunition," was traced to a Thomas Street cottage and called upon to surrender.

Wheed's answer was a burst of gunfire. Armed with rifles and revolvers he waged a furious two-hour battle with an army of 250 police before deciding to surrender. Therien was soon picked up near Ottawa, Kansas. Asciutto made good his escape and apparently returned to his native Italy.

Brought before a jury, Wheed admitted leadership of a gang with a long record of robbery and murder. He was sentenced to death; Carrao and Therien to imprisonment.

A substantial part of the payroll had been in gold coins. More than a thousand dollars worth were recovered from Wheed and an accomplice; sizeable amounts from the other two bandits.

One immediate outcome of this brutal murder was the establishment of the Chicago Crime Commission, a body which gained national recognition and is still functioning effectively today. Another was a prompt strengthening of security measures by Brink's. New plans were developed for covering the messenger at all times, and the first experiments were undertaken in armoring the sides of the open touring cars then in use. The "trailer" system was also instituted whereby a second car carrying armed guards followed the vehicle with the messenger and money. Brink's also offered a standing reward to all employes of $1000 for killing a bandit, $500 for wounding one. In later years these rewards were doubled.

That the new security measures had value was made

evident when the next attempt occurred to hold up a payroll guarded by Brink's.

About two years after the Winslow tragedy, a payroll of almost $10,000 was being delivered to the Hart, Schaffner & Marx office on 22nd Street in Chicago. As the money was being carried into the building, a gang of bandits appeared, but the Brink's men were not to be taken by surprise. In a lively exchange of gunfire, one of the bandits was killed and another wounded. A third managed to escape with only a small part of the payroll.

By the beginning of the 20's, Brink's was carrying money in vehicles that strangely resembled a school bus though the windows were protected by horizontal steel bars. These vehicles were followed by an open touring car with a belt of armor around its body. Such a convoy, usually a Model "T" Ford, was somewhat ironically nicknamed a "greyhound" by the crews. Though no robberies occurred, the Company pushed ahead with its development program and had vehicles with armored bodies on the streets as early as 1923.

Of course, the armored car cannot protect crew members once they have dismounted, nor give them effective support once they are out of firing range of the men remaining in the car.

On October 24, 1924 a Brink's crew was about to pay off some Otis Elevator Company men who were installing equipment in a partially completed building at 40th and Broadway, New York City. Robbers attacked without warning. Messenger Franklin Good was shot in the back, and the payroll valise was snatched from under his body by one of the bandits. Guard John Callanan exchanged shots with the attackers and then pursued the man who had seized the money. As he was about to grapple with

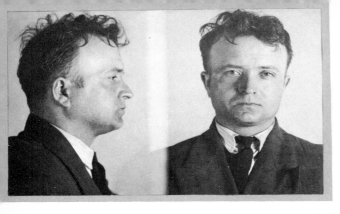

This police "mug" shot of Jawarski at least suggests why one of the toughest of killers was once known as the "angel of the choir." Photo was made after the Library Road dynamiting described below.

the bandit, the latter dropped the valise and shot Callanan through the nose, the bullet lodging in his cheekbone. Though badly wounded, Callanan recovered the payroll and the holdup gang fled. The wounded Brink's men were both taken to Bellevue Hospital where Good died the following day. Both of these courageous men hold high places on Brink's honor list.

The Dynamiting on the Library Road

In March 1927, in the Pennsylvania hills about 20 miles from Pittsburgh, there occurred the most spectacular robbery in the early history of Brink's.

An ex-choir boy named Paul Jawarski was then the leader and chief trigger man of a gang of hoodlums with a long tally of major crimes on its record. Because of the shape of Jawarski's head, the group was widely known as the Flathead Gang.

These men had carefully plotted and timed the weekly movement of a Brink's armored car and its convoy between the Pittsburgh office and the Terminal Coal Company at Coverdale.

Holing up in the farmhouse of an accomplice named Weckoski, the bandits had concealed access to a lonely road on the payroll route. With lengths of pipe loaded with high explosive, they mined two sections of the road and carried separate lead wires to electric detonators concealed in a pit at the edge of a bordering wood. On the 11th of March some nine members of the Flatheads were ready. They cut the phone wires to hamper communication with the police and took their posts.

The Brink's armored car appeared on schedule with its convoy car of armed guards close behind. As the armored car neared the far end of the mined section, one blast was touched off. The three-ton armored car was tossed into the air and landed upside down. A second blast, intended to catch the convoy car, was premature. However, the convoy car plunged into the crater torn in the road and was buried by falling debris and wrecked.

By some miracle, none of the Brink's men was seriously injured, but all were temporarily knocked out—and this saved them from death at the hands of the ambush gang. In mere minutes, the Flatheads were able to gather up the valises of payroll envelopes containing slightly less than $104,000 and make their escape to the hideout. They counted and divided the loot, took their shares and all but Jawarski left the district.

In a few minutes after the explosion, the Brink's guards

At left is the convoy car, wrecked by plunging into a hole blasted in the road. Below is the armored car tossed upside down by the explosion. It seems miraculous that no crewman was badly injured.

had recovered and spread the alarm. Again the work of police and insurance investigators was prompt and efficient. On the second day, Jawarski, fully armed but asleep in a bed, was covered and arrested on the Weckoski farm although he claimed to be a visitor named John Smith. In spite of his toughness, he chose to confess, implicated the other members of the gang and told where $38,000 of the money was buried. Exactly one month after the crime, he was convicted and sentenced to jail. Tried on a murder charge in connection with another payroll robbery, he was sentenced to death but managed, with another prisoner, to shoot his way out of jail.

After a year of liberty spent in more robberies, Jawarski—who ultimately confessed to 26 murders—was seriously injured in a gun battle with police in Detroit, Michigan, and was ultimately taken back to Pittsburgh and executed. Other members of the gang were apprehended and given jail sentences or condemned to death on murder charges.

Again the crime revealed a weakness in the early armored car—its wooden frame and floor. This led to the redesign of Brink's armored cars incorporating an all steel frame and armored steel floor. Obviously, no armored car can be made completely invulnerable—even an army tank is not. However, the strength and security of the modern armored car is evidenced by the fact that no robbery due to structural weakness of a Brink's armored car has occurred since 1927.

On March 22, 1935, five bandits attempted a payroll holdup at the offices of the Chicago meat packers, Wilson & Co., Inc. At the time Brink's was in the process of turning over unclaimed envelopes to the Wilson cashier. One of the bandits broke the glass into the cashier's office and shouted "Hands up." Seeing two armed Brink's employees, Edgar Buzzo and Peter J. Ries, the bandit aimed his sawed off shotgun pointblank at Buzzo and pulled the trigger. Fortunately his gun misfired. Instantly both Buzzo and Ries, ready for just such emergencies, opened fire and the robber fell to the floor seriously wounded. The other three bandits immediately fled the building and escaped in their waiting car driven by the fifth bandit. The wounded bandit was subsequently sentenced to a term of 1 to 14 years in prison.

Five bandits, attempting a payroll robbery at Eastman Kodak Company, Chicago, on December 18, 1947, were also driven off by an alert and courageous Brink's crew.

A particularly tragic robbery occurred on June 25, 1949. Four bandits planned the robbery of a Brink's crew at the South Chicago Savings Bank. One of them named Jakalski, armed with a sub-machine gun in a paper sack, waited with an accomplice on a stairway of the building. When Messenger Joseph Den and Guard Joseph Koziol appeared, both were murdered in cold blood. The loot was only $920 in cash with $377,000 in bank-endorsed, non-negotiable checks.

Three of the bandits were arrested within the following month, and Jakalski was then picked up in a Cheyenne, Wyoming, railroad yard as a vagrant, recognized and extradited to Chicago. Twice juries refused to convict him on a murder charge, but Brink's and their insurance company pressed the case relentlessly. In February, 1951, Jakalski was sentenced to 199 years on the Federal charge of robbing a member bank of the Federal Reserve System.

On July 8, 1951, a Brink's crew called at the plant of the Bowman Dairy Company in Chicago. Messenger Ebert and Guard Kobylinski on a routine pickup entered

J. D. Allen, then President, giving awards to Brink's crewmen who fought off bandits, killing two, in attempted Bowman Dairy Co. robbery. From left: Messenger Emmet Ebert, Guard Theodore Kobylinski, Driver Julius Blanchart.

the plant while Driver Blanchart remained with the car. Three bandits dressed in butcher smocks attacked Blanchart and slugged him with a shotgun butt. In spite of this, he killed one of the bandits and wounded another. Ebert and Kobylinski came racing to his aid and killed the wounded bandit. The third man escaped. No money was lost.

That same summer, Brink's crewmen entered the Biltmore Theatre in Toronto, Canada, to pick up the receipts. Suspicious of a man hurrying out of the theatre, they took note of his appearance. When they learned from the manager that he had just been robbed, one of the Brink's men pursued the robber through the streets, collared him and recovered the $900 that had been stolen.

On October 26, 1951, another example of fine courage occurred in Chicago. Messenger Ervin Cisar was making a regular stop at the Economy Currency Exchange when he observed a man standing in the cashier's cage with manager Sam Bianco. Suspicious of the situation, Cisar asked who the visitor was. The man replied that he was a relative, at the same time nudging the manager in the back with a gun hidden in his pocket. Bianco warned Cisar by stepping on his toe. Cisar instantly covered the bandit with his revolver and held him for the police.

On November 13, 1952, a Brink's crew entering the Canadian Bank of Commerce at Walkerville, Ontario, surprised two bandits in the act of holding up the bank. Twenty-two bank employes were handcuffed and lying on the floor. The Brink's men drove off the bandits and pursued them, but they made their escape by commandeering a passing car. No money was lost by the bank.

The Attempt on the Canadian Race Track Funds

On the evening of August 3, 1955, a Brink's armored car left the Buffalo Branch to pick up the day's receipts at the Fort Erie race track in Ontario. In the vehicle were Messenger Clohessy and Driver Kemp accompanied by Guards Klodzinski and Thompson.

At the track, the crew picked up six padlocked boxes containing $498,500 and returned to the Branch which was, at that hour, closed for the night. Taking reasonable precautions but not following the full security procedure, Clohessy entered, checked the premises, went to the turret, admitted the armored car and closed the door. Then the "once in a million" chance occurred.

Three bandits had broken into the garage and concealed themselves. When the crew men got out of their car, they found themselves covered by a sub-machine gun and pistols. Clohessy, observing this from the turret, touched off the ADT and howler alarms, drew his revolver and went to the door of the check-in room to help his

'Why Al and Bud, Come Right In!'

Cartoon on Walkerville incident is from the Windsor, Ontario *Daily Star.*

Scene in the street minutes after the second bandit had been driven from the house by tear gas. Note police wiping eyes. Man at extreme left is Guard Thompson.

comrades. As he opened the door, he was met by a burst of sub-machine gun fire that put a slug in his right chest. Stunned, he was able to close and bolt the door, then crawl to the turret and phone the police.

Frightened by the alarm, the bandits hurriedly grabbed two of the six money boxes from the armored car and fled. Leaving Kemp behind to attend Clohessy, Thompson and Klodzinski rearmed themselves and rushed outside. One money box was lying in the street. A bandit running down the street was carrying the other. The guards exchanged shots with him, then jumped in Klodzinski's car and gave chase. Within a block, they found the other money box in the street, retrieved it and resumed pursuit of the bandits who were now fleeing in a car. Police joined the chase, the bandits were driven from their car and two of them captured in houses where they had taken refuge. The two are serving 15 to 60 year terms after conviction on first degree robbery charges. Up to now the third bandit has not been apprehended.

Additional incidents could be cited in which Brink's

86

crewmen acquitted themselves well. In other instances when not themselves the object of attack, they broke up attempted robberies and captured or assisted in the capture of bandits.

Detailed in this chapter, and in the second following devoted to the Boston robbery, the amount of violence looms large. But it should be remembered that these, and the very few other robberies in Brink's history, occurred over a period of nearly 70 years during which many thousands of billions of dollars were transported safely and uneventfully. And, of course, no customer has ever lost a penny, through robbery or from any other cause, of funds entrusted to Brink's care.

Brink's men—one of them carrying nothing but value-less bank clearings—have been slain in the line of duty. Yet the records unmistakably show that being a member of an armored car crew is a relatively safe occupation. Insurance companies with many years of actuarial experience to guide them, have for some time insured these men at standard rates. No "hazardous occupation" premiums are charged such as apply to certain classes of construction workers, policemen, truck drivers and miners—jobs that many people would consider relatively prosaic.

Brink's crewmen, through strict adherence to the "book of rules," have as long life expectancies as do salesmen, lawyers, teachers or other unarmed workers.

CHAPTER IX

More Branches, Stockholders, Services

IF THE THREAD that runs through this history of Brink's seems broken at times, it is because of the need to group certain related events rather than to follow a strict chronological sequence. Actually, there was no definite hiatus in the consistent progress of the Company.

The tempo of business naturally varies. After the depth of the depression, the opening of new branches was resumed though not as rapidly as in the twenties. It slowed again during World War II, then got back into stride and reached a total of 100 branches on July 1, 1954 with the opening of an office at Regina, Saskatchewan.

Shades of Perry Brink! Even the optimistic founder never could have dreamed that some day his one wagon, one horse outfit would grow to an international institution and his name become a household word.

And still more expansion. In 1957 Southern Armored Service, Inc. was acquired to amplify operations in the state of Florida. The very latest office to open was at Sherbrooke, Quebec, on February 2, 1959—the 112th branch in the United States and Canada.

* * *

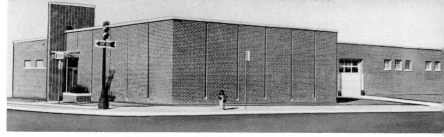
New Brink's Branch building at Kansas City, Missouri.

1934 was the 75th anniversary of the Company and was marked by two unusual events. Another book about Brink's was published titled "The Romance of Moving Money," again by the well-known author, Forrest Crissey. And the corporate name was changed from Brink's Express Company simply to Brink's, Incorporated. This matter was handled by a young lawyer named Eugene E. Murphy who had succeeded William English as Secretary and General Counsel of the Company, and who was destined ultimately for its presidency. For a time Mr. Murphy retained his partnership in Harrold, Quilici, Clementi & Murphy, withdrawing from this firm only when he found his widening duties with Brink's demanded his full time.

In a certain sense, it can be said that a company comes of age financially when it broadens its base of ownership by offering stock to the public. In the case of Brink's, this occurred in May 1937.

With the steady growth of the Company, the two Allens realized that continued family ownership posed certain hazards, not only to the business but to their own estates, should sickness or accident befall either or both principals. They felt that a general strengthening would result if key employes and the investing public participated in stock ownership.

An offering was made through Washburn and Company, Inc. of 17,000 shares. Employes were afforded an opportunity to purchase a limited amount of stock on favorable terms at a slightly lower price than the public

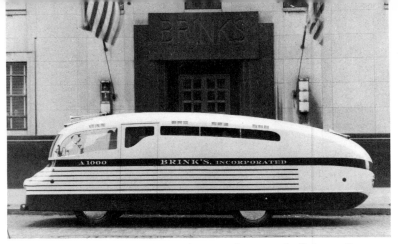

This elaborate, experimental armored car was built in 1946.

offering. In both instances, the stock was purchased from Frank Allen and J. D. Allen. The issue was subscribed for promptly and some years later was split 4 for 1.

From its incorporation in 1879 Brink's has had an unusual financial record. In good times and bad, in the depths of depressions and through three wars, the Company managed to earn a profit. Sometimes it was small but it always permitted the payment of dividends. Only once, in 1891, was the dividend paid in stock rather than in cash.

Late in the '30s the business tempo quickened prior to the entry of the United States into World War II. After Pearl Harbor, manpower such as Brink's desired was at a premium and vehicles became irreplaceable. Yet, during the war years, Company personnel performed prodigies in paying off huge numbers of workers at ship yards, government construction jobs, munitions companies and aircraft factories. Many office and money room men were replaced by women, and armored car crews gave their time generously to bond drives and other patriotic activities.

* * *

At various points in this book, you have read about specific services provided by Brink's. For example, payroll handling in Chapters II, III and IV; bank service in Chapter V; removals in Chapter VI; pickup and deposit, and safes in Chapter VII. There are other important services that should be outlined in order to make this book complete.

Serving the "Fed"

To bankers and Brink's men, it's the "Fed." To the man in the street, it's a super banking system that in various mysterious ways affects the entire economy of our country.

The Federal Reserve System has been in operation since 1913. The country has been divided into twelve districts conveniently demarcated for business purposes. In each of these there is a Federal Reserve bank, and there are also twenty-four branches throughout the United States. Every National bank must be a member of the System; State banks that qualify are eligible for membership. Member banks actually own the capital stock of the Reserve bank in their district and have representation on the board of directors.

The ever increasing volume of money being handled through the Federal Reserve System is naturally resulting in a heavier movement of funds between the Federal Reserve Banks and member banks.

Though Brink's had performed services for various

Brink's armored cars were specially painted with War Bond messages during World War II. Many crewmen contributed time to patriotic activities.

A Brink's armored car in front of the Federal Reserve on Chicago's La Salle Street.

Federal Reserve Banks as early as 1932, its first regular "Fed" runs were made October 11, 1949 under contract with the Federal Reserve Bank of Cleveland and were known as Akron runs #1 and #2.

The service has grown rapidly and is continuing to do so. Curtailment of train service to smaller communities and the discontinuance of some branch line trains entirely are major reasons the Federal Reserve is employing the armored car more and more.

The service also provides a number of advantages. Schedules are fast and well maintained. Door-to-door delivery eliminates the need for the member banks to send employes to the express or post office to pick up or deliver shipments. This saves time and, more important, removes the threat to personal safety and possible loss of the money through holdup.

As of the end of 1958, over a hundred Federal Reserve runs served approximately 1500 banks. Armored car runs in this work usually involve round trips of 200 to 500 miles per day.

Brink's armored cars perform services at key cities for the Bank of Canada, the institution that functions in the Dominion much as the Federal Reserve does in the United States. Brink's also serves the seven chartered banks that provide Canada's banking facilities.

. . . and the Mint

One of the newest Brink's services is that provided for the Bureau of the Mint, a sub-department of the United States Treasury. The Mint produces copper, nickel and silver coins; paper currency comes from the Treasury's Bureau of Printing and Engraving.

The first run made for the United States Mint was on June 28, 1954 when Brink's hauled one million dollars in coin from the Cincinnati branch to the Federal Reserve Bank of Cleveland. Subsequently, contracts have been signed with the General Services Administration for a series of Mint runs.

Since the inception of service for the United States Mint, Brink's continues to move coin from Philadelphia, Denver and San Francisco to Federal Reserve banks. Because coin is heavy and bulky, most Mint runs are made with special, armored tractor-trailer combinations.

The greatest single withdrawal was 145,000 pounds of silver from the Denver Mint. It was moved by Brink's to Federal Reserve Banks at El Paso and Dallas, Texas, Kansas City, Missouri, and Minneapolis, Minnesota.

Although Brink's people will not discuss their services for the "Fed" or the Mint in any detail, it is not hard to detect that they are proud to have been chosen as a carrier by these two great governmental institutions.

Armored truck-trailer combination at the Denver Mint.

Brink's largest vehicles have radio-telephones for communication en route.

Clearing House Service

For many years, Brink's has played an important role in this banking activity. The Company serves banks by picking up their check clearings and transporting them to the clearing house by armored car. In Chicago, where the service is more complete than anywhere else, more than 60 banks with clearings of $200,000,000 are served in this manner and Brink's usually has 76 men, including four supervisors, and 24 armored cars at the Clearing House each morning. All men except the drivers work inside.

It goes like this. Each bank gives Brink's a signed check made out to the Clearing House. After the clearings are taken to the Clearing House they are sorted as to banks, and the amount of balance each bank owes is determined. The Brink's messenger then fills in the check for the amount of the balance and turns it over to the Clearing House. Next, crews return promptly to each bank with checks drawn on it for speedy posting.

The service saves time for banks, prevents theft of check clearings and eliminates risk to bank employes. Though valueless in themselves, clearings, when not transported by armored car, have been stolen in the belief that they represent cash. When theft has occurred it has resulted in a serious disruption of business, much extra work and considerable financial loss.

Parking Meters

Here is another of the complications arising in the automobile age. A great many cities and towns derive additional income from the coins placed in parking meters. In some places, these funds are now being used to finance parking lots and garages in congested areas.

Two Brink's men making a regular parking meter collection.
The scene here is Montreal, Quebec.

The first parking meter service by Brink's was introduced in Milwaukee, Wisconsin in December, 1949.
Since that time Brink's collection services have been
employed by many cities in somewhat varying forms. In
Milwaukee, armored cars and crews using special equipment pick up the coins and deposit them in banks designated by the city.

The Comptroller of the City of Milwaukee, in writing
to the City Traffic Engineer of Atlanta, Georgia, said in
part: "May I state categorically at this point that there
never has been any question of the safety, surety and
dependability of the Brink's service. We are completely
satisfied and would remain so even in the presence of a
competing agency."

In Chicago, for example, the handling is different.
Meter coins are picked up and hauled back to the
Branch. There the money passes through automatic coin
sorting machines which separate and count the various
denominations. They are then wrapped and used by
Brink's for its change service. As a final step, Brink's

sends a check to the City covering the total amount.

The City Collector of Chicago wrote in a letter to Brink's: "We feel that this service is the most satisfactory and efficient method of handling funds from parking meters; and also the cost of this service is far less than the cost would be if the City of Chicago used its own employes to perform this operation.

"In closing, I would like to add that we are well satisfied with the service you are performing, and we are looking forward to many more years of pleasant business relations with your organization."

People in conversation with Brink's officials often ask about slugs in the meters. Brink's men say that many dodges are used ranging from folded up foil gum wrappers to buttons and slugs. Rarely do these substitutes for coins work. Usually they jam the meter so no one can use it and often make costly repairs necessary at the taxpayers' expense. Brink's points out one bright spot—many a nickel or dime goes into a meter when a penny would have bought all the time needed.

The platform at the rear of this armored car is hydraulically operated for moving heavily loaded hand trucks between car floor and street level.

CHAPTER X

The Million Dollar Robbery

JANUARY 17, 1950 was a routine winter evening in the Boston Branch. Shortly after seven o'clock, five Brink's employees were at work in the vault room. Secure in the belief they were protected by the time-tested safety precautions of the Branch, the men were calmly checking shipments of money brought in that day in the normal course of business.

Suddenly a voice spoke:

"This is a stickup. Open the gate and don't give us any trouble."

The startled Brink's men looked up to see seven strange figures standing outside the steel cage, each with a leveled pistol. The figures were dressed alike in sailors' pea jackets and visored caps, and each wore a grotesque, rubber Hallowe'en mask.

Refusal to obey the command would have meant death. The gate was opened, five bandits rushed in, ordered the Brink's men to lie on the floor, bound them hand and foot and covered their mouths with strips of adhesive tape.

Within twenty minutes the bandits had stuffed stacks of sealed packages into large sea bags they had brought with them and were gone.

At 7:36 P.M. an alarm sounded in the American

District Telegraph office. One of the victims had managed to press a button which set off the alarm.

Three minutes later police cars were at the scene. Seven minutes later roadblocks had been set on all highways leading out of Boston, and the police of 14 states had been alerted. In spite of all this, the bandits escaped the police net.

That is the bare outline of phase one of the robbery of Brink's Boston office in which $1,219,000 in cash and about an equal amount in checks and securities were taken. It was the biggest robbery in history and destined to become the most celebrated in American crime annals. What followed formed a long and complex story of which only the highlights can be given here.

Eugene E. Murphy, then Vice President, Secretary and General Counsel of Brink's, Otto Plank, Vice President-Operations, and H. Edward Reeves, representing Brink's insurance underwriters, flew to Boston as soon as the news was flashed over the wire, and were active in the investigation that followed. These men moved swiftly to establish the exact amount of the loss and to see that it was made good immediately.

Naturally the police and the press gave consideration to the theory that it was an inside job. The Brink's men on duty were Thomas B. Lloyd, James Allen, Charles Grell, Sherman Smith and Herman Pfaff. All had good records and told straightforward stories of the crime. All took lie detector tests and were cleared of complicity. Company officials avowed their faith in them.

Identification by the victims was impossible because the faces of the bandits were completely covered by masks. They were much alike in size, similarly dressed and left no fingerprints because they wore gloves.

Clues were scanty. A visored cap with the maker's name torn out had been left behind. It was never traced. There were some pieces of adhesive tape and 32 short lengths of rope which had been used to bind the victims.

With these meager leads there began a manhunt ranking with the most intensive criminal investigations in history. The Boston police, the Suffolk County District Attorney's office, the Office of the State of Massachusetts Attorney General, the Massachusetts State Police and the Federal Bureau of Investigation joined in the hunt.

Brink's offered a reward of $100,000 for information leading to the arrest and conviction of the robbers.

Tips and theories poured in. Within a few days of the robbery, the Boston police had received 10,000 letters. Brink's still has in its archives a large box of letters sent to the Boston Branch or the Home Office from all over the country as well as from Germany, Belgium, Honduras, Guatemala, Brazil and Netherlands West Indies. Amateur sleuths, hungry for fame and the reward, converged on Boston from all points.

Nothing came of all this.

Interviewing people known to have been in the vicinity of Brink's office on the night of the crime was slightly more productive. Police turned up a witness who said he had seen six or seven men drive away from Brink's in a stake truck with a green cover.

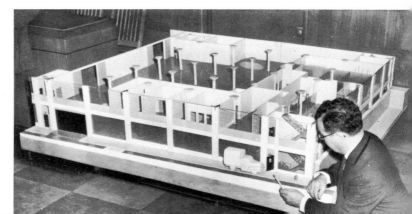

heriff Fred R. Sullivan iews model of Brink's Boson offices used during the ial of the robbers in Suflk Superior Court. Mod-l, now exhibited by F.B.I. n Washington, D.C., iows garage pillars, stairays, doors, offices, count-ig desks and open vault. *Associated Press photo.*

In a Stoughton dump, pieces of a stake truck were found which had been cut up with a welding torch. All numbers had been burned off—except one. From it, police established that the truck had been stolen. They theorized that it was the getaway truck, and its destruction suggested the care the robbers had taken to cover their tracks.

Children found two pistols on a local beach. One pistol was thrown away and lost. The other was recovered by the police and proved to be one of the guns taken from Brink's office. No other clues turned up. Newspaper reporters had little to go on, and the case began to look like a dead end. Was this the perfect crime? Would the perpetrators of the robbery never be discovered?

During November, 1952, a Federal Grand Jury was convened in Boston, Massachusetts, and the government presented evidence in an effort to obtain indictments against seven individuals who were alleged to have participated in the Brink's robbery. For the next seven weeks witnesses were brought before the Grand Jury in an effort to obtain indictments before the expiration of the Federal statute of limitation on January 17, 1953. However, the Jury refused to return any indictments. It openly expressed its discouragement in not being able to indict the suspects rounded up by an intensive search following a detailed investigation. The Grand Jury of 22 men and 1 woman said it could return no indictments because the bandits were effectively disguised; there was a shortage of witnesses; "certain" witnesses had refused to testify, and the Grand Jury would not force them to do so.

Years passed. Each anniversary of the holdup, newspapers reprinted the story and reported that the solution was still a mystery.

District Attorney Garrett H. Byrne, left, is shown here questioning
Joseph J. "Specs" O'Keefe, at right. *Associated Press photo.*

A revival occurred when a long-hunted bank bandit
was taken into custody as a suspect, but he proved to
have an iron-clad alibi. Once more the case dropped
from the front pages.

Suddenly, odd things began to happen. "Specs"
O'Keefe, a Boston underworld figure, was ambushed on
the street by a man later identified as "Trigger" Burke,
a New York gunman. "Trigger" missed. O'Keefe was
ambushed again and this time was wounded in the wrist.

Rumors circulated that O'Keefe was one of the
Brink's bandits; that he was threatening to talk because
he had been cheated out of $60,000 of his share of the
loot; that his erstwhile pals had hired Burke to silence
him with death. The wall of silence and obscurity was
beginning to crack.

O'Keefe, in and out of jail on other charges, was
questioned intensively by law enforcement authorities.
And at last he talked. On January 12, 1956, six years
lacking five days after the robbery occurred, the FBI

released an announcement that the case had been solved.

It was just in time. In five days, the Massachusetts statute of limitations would have forever prevented prosecution of the bandits. The Federal statute of limitations had already run its course barring prosecution under Federal law.

The FBI named 11 men as principals in the crime. Eight, including O'Keefe, were taken into custody and two more were soon arrested. One of the 11, Joseph F. Bansfield, had died of natural causes.

Arrested were Joseph F. McGinnis, Anthony Pino, Adolph Maffie, James I. Faherty, Thomas F. Richardson, Henry D. Baker, Michael V. Geagan, Vincent J. Costa, Stanley H. Gusciora and O'Keefe. All had criminal records.

Brink's officials were jubilant. J. D. Allen, then Chairman of the Board, and H. E. Reeves, then President, wired J. Edgar Hoover:

> "Our congratulations and appreciation for the work you and your fine organization have done in apprehending the robbers responsible for the Brink's Boston holdup . . . Only through the untiring efforts and tenaciousness of your entire staff could this difficult task have been accomplished . . . Our country is indeed fortunate to have so efficient an organization and splendid personnel protecting the safety of its citizens . . . There was never any doubt in our minds but that your organization would ultimately bring the criminals to justice . . . You have the sincere thanks of our entire organization."
>
> (*signed*)
> J. D. ALLEN, *Chairman of the Board*
> H. E. REEVES, *President*

UNITED STATES DEPARTMENT OF JUSTICE

FEDERAL BUREAU OF INVESTIGATION

WASHINGTON 25, D. C.

January 13, 1956

Mr. J. D. Allen
Chairman of the Board
Brink's, Inc.
234 East 24th Street
Chicago, Illinois

Dear Mr. Allen:

Many thanks for the very kind telegram of yesterday afternoon from Mr. H. Edward Reeves and you. You may be sure that my associates and I most deeply appreciate your thoughtfulness in sending this message concerning our investigation of the Brink's Boston Robbery.

Your confidence in our organization is most encouraging, and your generous comments mean a lot to all of us in the FBI.

Sincerely yours,

J. Edgar Hoover

Above is J. Edgar Hoover's reply to the Brink's telegram.

The men were indicted by the Grand Jury on the testimony of O'Keefe who pleaded guilty to the charges and became the State's principal witness. Gusciora died in jail before the trial began leaving eight men to face the court.

Eight of the defendants in the Brink's robbery gathered in a guarded room at Superior Court. Left to right are Anthony Pino, James I. Faherty, Henry Baker, Adolph Maffie, Thomas F. Richardson, Michael V. Ceagan, Vincent J. Costa, and Joseph F. McGinnis. At far right is defense counsel Paul Smith. *Associated Press photo.*

After months of delaying actions by Paul T. Smith, chief defense attorney, and his aides who filed 1,200 motions in behalf of their clients, trial began in the Superior Court of Massachusetts at Boston on August 6, 1956 with Judge Felix Forte presiding. The prosecution was headed by District Attorney Garrett H. Byrne who was aided by assistant District Attorneys Frederick T. Doyle and John McAuliffe.

Because of the wide publicity given the case, it required nearly four weeks to select a jury, and more than 1,700 talesmen were questioned before the all-male panel was complete.

O'Keefe, a highly articulate man, proved a strong witness for the state. He told in detail the amazingly painstaking, long-range planning of the robbery, including the procuring of keys to the building, and named all of the defendants as participants. Seven, he said, committed the actual robbery, others played roles as lookouts and one drove the getaway truck. McGinnis, pictured as the "brains" of the gang, was not at the robbery scene but in a liquor store he operated, talking to a city detective and thus establishing an alibi.

The defense failed to shake O'Keefe's story. None of the defendants took the stand, and defense testimony consisted largely of alibi and character witnesses.

After a trial lasting 42 days, the jury returned a verdict of guilty against all defendants on October 6. On the 9th Judge Felix Forte passed sentence giving seven of the defendants life terms in prison with additional sentences ranging from 8 years to life to be served concurrently. McGinnis was sentenced to serve eight life terms running concurrently. In addition, all defendants were given two-year terms for conspiracy, not to be served concurrently, which they will also have to serve if given parole. In dismissing the jury, Judge Forte praised its courage. The firm action of both judge and jury received wide acclaim in the press.

On October 10, the eight convicted men were taken to Massachusetts state prison at Walpole. O'Keefe, who pleaded guilty, was remanded to East Cambridge jail to await later sentencing. Defense counsel entered an appeal. Oral arguments were heard on Feb. 11, 1959 before the Supreme Judicial Court of Massachusetts.[1] No decision had been rendered at the time this book went to press.

What Happened to the Money?

On June 4, 1956 a routine arrest was made in Baltimore, Maryland, which led to the first sizable recovery of the money taken. One Jordan Perry, an ex-convict, had proffered a moldy, crumbling and weather-streaked $10

[1]On July 1, 1959 convictions were affirmed.

State Police armed with riot guns guard the eight prisoners leaving the court van at Massachusetts State Prison, Walpole, to begin life sentences for the Brink's robbery committed nearly seven years earlier. *Associated Press photo.*

bill in payment of 25¢ worth of shots in a shooting gallery. The attendant became suspicious of the bill and turned it over to the police. An examination disclosed that its serial number was that of one of the missing bills. Perry was taken into custody. Several other missing bills were found in his pockets and a cache of $4635 was found under a rug in his Baltimore hotel room. Perry was questioned by the Federal Bureau of Investigation and, within 18 hours of his arrest, the FBI and the Boston police found $54,548 behind a false wall in the owner's office in the basement of a Boston south end apartment, wrapped in newspapers and plastic bags, and stored in an old refrigerator. The money was moldy and rotting and had the appearance of having been buried. All of it was identified by serial numbers as part of the missing cash.

The Federal Bureau of Investigation arrested John F. Buccelli, owner of the building, and Edward A. Bennett, a known pal of "Specs" O'Keefe. The three men arrested for having illegal possession of the money were not connected with the robbery itself. Two of them—"Fats" Buccelli and "Wimpy" Bennett received jail sentences; Perry was convicted and sentenced on other charges.

The rest of the money has never been recovered. Police investigators are satisfied that none of the robbers showed sudden signs of affluence in the six years between crime and arrest. All lived modestly; some worked as laborers. No new apartments, no solid gold Cadillacs, no mink coats for wives or girl friends.

Various theories have been evolved to account for this oddity. A writer for the Boston Globe points out that the loot, divided among 11 bandits, amounted only to $16,000 per year per man and that this could easily have been spent gambling at race tracks, in card and dice games. Other writers suggest that the money never appeared because it is still in hiding. In support, they cite certain facts that are difficult to account for as coincidences.

"Fats" Buccelli was shot to death on June 19, 1958. That same day a New York gangster named Johnny Earle came to a similar violent end in a cafeteria. The connection? Earle and Buccelli had met the preceding day and both were former friends of the notorious "Trigger" Burke. Did gangland believe that these two had information about the hidden money?

Four other men alleged to have been involved in some way in the Boston robbery, have vanished or died by violence. They include George R. Killeen, Carlton M. O'Brien, George D. O'Brien and William Cameron. All the known criminals are in jail. With such evidence at

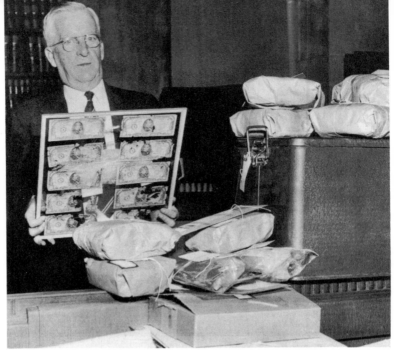

Court Clerk William Prendible with $54,548 of the Brink's money.
Note fragile condition of some bills. *Associated Press photo*.

hand it seems reasonable to cast a vote for the truth of
the adage that crime does not pay.

The solution of the Boston robbery exploded the myth
that this was the perfect crime. The relentless search gave
warning to criminals that no matter how painstaking the
planning, how clever the execution of a crime, the perpetrators will ultimately be brought to justice. The sober-
ing effect this knowledge might have on juvenile delin-
quents hoping to emulate the Boston bandits was especially
satisfying to Brink's officials and law enforcement officers.
Another source of satisfaction to Brink's was the fact that
Company employes were entirely cleared of any suspicion in connection with the robbery.

Manager Herbert Humphrey is still in charge of the
Boston Branch. Of the five men present at the robbery,
two have retired, three are still employed by Brink's.

It never should have happened. That it did can be blamed largely on human failure to live up to the letter of the book of rules.

Brink's promptly instituted a thorough review of its security procedures and spent more than half a million dollars improving the security, protective equipment and alarm systems of its Branches.

Customers at Boston, of course, were fully protected by Brink's insurance and completely reimbursed.

* * *

Brink's officials point out that every robbery detailed here and in Chapter VIII served at least one common end: to further tighten the security of the Company.

Each time, quick and careful studies were made to determine whether the robbery or assault had pinpointed a failure of the human element, a lapse in adherence to the rules, a weakness in Branch office protection or in the armored cars and equipment.

Each time, appropriate steps were taken, whether this meant substantially re-building an office, altering the design of the vehicles, changing an operating procedure or establishing a flying squad of security supervisors to check practices throughout the organization.

Ten-wheel, diesel powered armored car used for over-the-road runs shown on Chicago's Outer Drive.

CHAPTER XI

Brink's in the Modern Era

FROM 1890 to 1953 Brink's Home Office occupied the premises at 711 West Monroe Street. By 1916 the transportation of money and valuables had become such an important part of the business that it was separated from the express operation and moved to the First National Bank Building. As the business expanded, new and larger quarters were occupied in 1918 in the Old Colony Building and in 1923 in a building built to Brink's specifications at 571 West Jackson Boulevard. In 1930 the rapidly dwindling express end of the business was sold to Marks Express and Teaming Company, except for two contracts retained by Brink's. Space thus released from use at 711 West Monroe was rented out.

By 1938 the money handling division had outgrown the 571 West Jackson premises and was returned to 711 West Monroe. This building was completely remodeled, modern offices and vaults with all necessary protective devices installed, and an adjoining lot and building, formerly used by the Railway Express Agency, was purchased. The building was torn down and a reinforced concrete garage and repair shop was constructed.

Entrance to the "old" Home Office at 711 West Monroe Street, Chicago.
Brink's occupied this site for 63 years.

In 1952 the new garage property was condemned to make way for a superhighway. The remainder of the property was sold to Dow, Jones & Company to house the editorial offices and presses of the *Wall Street Journal*. The building at 234 East 24th Street described in Chapter I was then purchased and remodeled to house the general offices, Chicago Branch and garage. The move was completed in May of 1953.

A "sister ship" of the armored car above pulls up in front of the new Home Office at 234 East 24th Street. Money, records and security items were moved in Brink's own vehicles.

Armored tractor and trailer used in Federal Reserve and Mint service.

In 1956 the Pittston Company bought 22.25% of the outstanding shares of Brink's, Incorporated and offered to buy, subject to the approval of the Interstate Commerce Commission, sufficient additional shares to give it control. Shareholders responded with tenders for sufficient additional shares to give Pittston control upon Interstate Commerce Commission approval. Application was then made to the Interstate Commerce Commission for authorization to complete the purchase. In its application, Pittston agrees that if the Interstate Commerce Commission grants approval, Pittston will also purchase, at the option price, the shares of any other Brink's shareholders who desire to sell. At the time of going to press with this book, the Interstate Commerce Commission had the application under consideration.[1]

On June 1, 1956, after 52 years of active service with Brink's, J. D. Allen resigned as Chairman of the Board of Directors and the position of Chairman was abolished. Mr. Allen remains a Director.

H. Edward Reeves, elected President in 1952, resigned Jan. 1st, 1957. He remains a Director and consultant.

Eugene E. Murphy succeeded Mr. Reeves as President, and is only the sixth man to hold that title in the long history of the Company. P. William Baddeley succeeded Mr. Murphy as Secretary.

[1]Application approved May 20, 1959.

Lunch time gives Brink's top officials an opportunity for informal discussion of business problems. From left to right are K. C. Allen, Vice President-Business Development, Otto Plank, Vice President-Operations, H. Edward Reeves, Consultant and Director, Charles W. Allen, Senior Vice President, P. William Baddeley, Vice President and Secretary, Eugene E. Murphy, President and Parker T. Jones, Treasurer.

The Company has continued its policy of bringing men up through the ranks. Brink's management is alive to the fact that the strength of a business lies largely in the depth of its personnel. As a result, special attention is given to those showing outstanding aptitude and they are moved up to administrative positions as openings occur.

In order to bring together everyone throughout the growing organization and maintain a "family" feeling, a house organ called the Brink's MESSENGER was launched in July 1952. This quarterly magazine contains personal news from the branches, items about various departments and company information of interest to all employes. It is liberally illustrated with photos of new buildings and vehicles, operational or personal snapshots and cartoons contributed by employes.

Since early in 1952, a system of awards for veteran employes has been in operation. At 25 years, a framed

Right, cover of a recent issue of the MESSENGER.
Below, cartoons contributed by Brink's employes.

YOU EVER BEEN "HELD UP" IN THIS CITY?

MISTER, THE ONLY PEOPLE WHO HOLD US UP ARE SOME OF OUR CUSTOMERS!

—*Drawn by C. Acton, Toronto*

"*I've had a funny feeling ever since he started following us.*"
—*by Driver Joseph F. Marshall, Cleveland Branch*

Brink's Messenger

FALL & WINTER, 1958

With the vault door opened wide, a vault man trundles out a load of coin and currency. Vaults at the branches are similar to those in larger banks.

Coins from parking meters in Chicago go into "Gravel Gertie" for denominating preparatory to wrapping.

Money room activities reach a peak before pay days. Many employes are women who have become highly skilled in handling money.

wall plaque with hand illuminated decorations, and a handsome wrist watch that carries on its band a gold replica of the Brink's shield engraved with the recipient's name and the words, "Twenty-five years of service." After 30 years, the employe also receives a gold lapel pin in the form of a Brink's shield and bearing an appropriate legend. 35 and 40-year veterans receive a similar emblem set with a diamond—a larger stone in the latter case— and mounted in a gold tie clip. In seven years 461 awards have been presented.

The names of the recipients of these awards as well as those given awards for safe driving or other meritorious service, are featured in each issue of the MESSENGER.

* * *

This history would not be complete without giving a fairly accurate idea of the scope of Brink's present operations.

Over one-half of all the armored cars operating on the streets and highways of the United States carry the Brink's shield and trademark. In six Canadian provinces, Brink's Express Company of Canada, Limited, operates an additional fleet of one hundred armored cars that are counterparts of those in the States.

It was stated earlier that, as of February 1959, Brink's

Newest of Brink's check cashing armored cars is called "Sputnik" by the crewmen. Check cashing is occasionally done in customer's garages during the winter months.

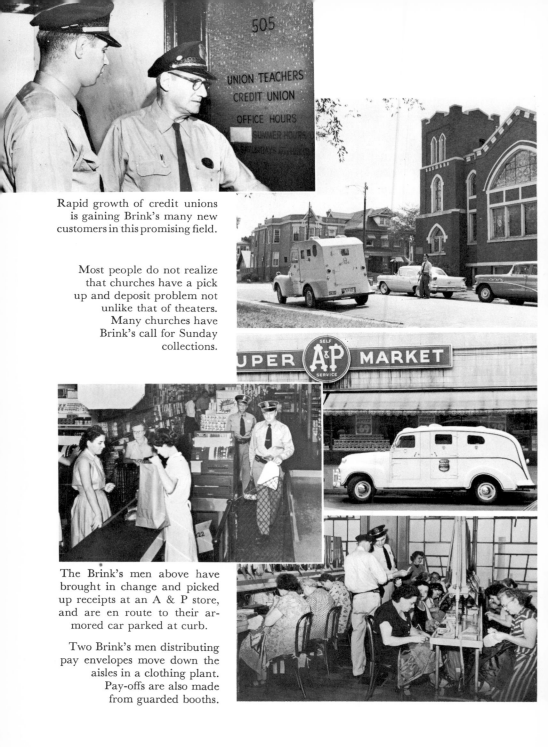

Rapid growth of credit unions is gaining Brink's many new customers in this promising field.

Most people do not realize that churches have a pick up and deposit problem not unlike that of theaters. Many churches have Brink's call for Sunday collections.

The Brink's men above have brought in change and picked up receipts at an A & P store, and are en route to their armored car parked at curb.

Two Brink's men distributing pay envelopes move down the aisles in a clothing plant. Pay-offs are also made from guarded booths.

had 112 branches and 1,026 armored cars handling an average of one and one-third billion dollars a day. In the course of this operation, Brink's armored cars make over 150,000 commercial service stops per week and over 31,000 bank stops. In a year, the armored cars run up a total of about 12,500,000 route miles.

Brink's check cashing service, provided by contract at the customer's place of business, converts an average of 11 million pay checks per year into cash. To provide the money for this service, Brink's obtains advances from customers, uses its own funds and must, in addition, borrow about half a billion dollars annually from banks.

Brink's officials point out—and their view is supported by law enforcement officers—that the danger of payroll robberies is eliminated when the Company's full protective payroll service is utilized, or the check cashing service described above is used. They also state that paying by check does not actually reduce crime but merely moves the scene of robberies to the stores or bars that carry extra money to cash pay checks, an accommodation provided when a purchase is made. This is substantiated by the fact that newspapers frequently report armed robberies occurring at such places.

The smooth and uninterrupted manner in which all of these operations are performed is more impressive when it is remembered that the Company handles only money and valuables. Every mile and every moment therefore have their hazards. Not the least of these is the powerful temptation for veteran crew members to regard a bag of money as no more than so many pounds to be lifted and carried. Years of uneventful service make it difficult to maintain the constant alertness that is the surest protection against danger. Yet it is evident from the records

A Brink's armor car takes San Francisco's steep Nob Hill in stri... One of the famo... cable cars can b... seen in the back ground. Photo courtesy of *Clues* magazine.

of the insurance underwriters that Brink's employes have consistently kept up the highest standards of security.

* * *

The Money Movers are very taciturn when it comes to talking about the details of their business—a reasonable attitude when you consider the nature of that business. It would hardly be prudent to tell a casual visitor sitting across the desk that the Company is at four that afternoon distributing a million dollar payroll at the XYZ plant; nor would it be wise to tell a group of acquaintances at the luncheon table that a ten million dollar shipment is in transit on Highway 66 near Tucumcari, New Mexico. For obvious reasons, names of customers, amounts of shipments and the routes to be used are all highly classified information.

As President Murphy puts it, "Most businessmen can gossip about the big things their company is doing—maybe brag a little. But the greater the job we are doing, the greater the need for silence."

Most of the specific operations described in this book obviously are past history. Names of customers have been mentioned only in cases where it is felt that no breach of security is involved.

Because it acts solely as a private contract carrier, Brink's is not in a position to do any general advertising. Yet, it is highly conscious of the need to keep the good will of the public due to the fact that the Company uses sidewalks, streets and highways in the conduct of much of its business.

Bearing this out is the unwritten code of Brink's crewmen: "In case of trouble, the safety of the public comes first; concern for fellow crewmen is second; the security of the shipment comes third." No shipment has been lost through following this code.

While not seeking publicity except on rare occasions, Brink's follows a policy of giving newsmen and others, information as long as it does not affect security. It has a set of rules to govern the 100-odd branch managers in local contacts with the press, TV and radio. The rules also govern relations with individuals who wish to tie in with Brink's for publicity purposes. Except in the case of spot news, all requests for information or cooperation are cleared through the home office.

Brink's name crops up in newscasts, armored cars appear in cartoons, and it's surprising the number of items, articles and editorials the clipping bureau clips each week. "She and her luggage are being delivered in 'Brink's' safety," writes a Hollywood columnist. Such mention is indicative of how Brink's is rapidly becoming a generic word denoting the ultimate in safe transit and delivery.

In addition to clippings, Company officers present an imposing stack of testimonials and endorsements not only from customers, but from officials who are interested in crime prevention. There are certain of these of which President Murphy is particularly proud.

Here is one from Virgil Peterson, Director of the Chicago Crime Commission:

> "The use of armored car services for the protection of money in transit is an effective method of crime prevention. Professional holdup men are much less apt to attempt a robbery when the money is protected by an armored car manned by armed guards."

And here is what Chicago's Police Commissioner, Timothy J. O'Connor had to say recently:

> "There are a good many things that make the functioning of a police department more difficult; very few that make it easier. High on the list of these few is the armored car service as performed by Brink's and similar companies in Chicago. Armored cars protect money on the move just as a bank protects money in storage or on deposit.
> "Guarding money in transit is not the proper function of the police nor are we organized to provide this protection. The armored car companies are so organized and, by the very nature of things, can perform this service with maximum efficiency and economy.
> "The situation in Chicago undoubtedly is comparable to that in other cities throughout the country. I feel that our people should look upon the armored car companies as real adjuncts to public safety."

The following brief excerpt taken from an extensive article that appeared in *Life* magazine June 25, 1945, suggests the status Brink's enjoys with the general public:

> "Many people who have seen its uniformed troops in operation believe that Brink's is a government organization like the FBI or Secret Service . . . (Brink's men) are licensed to carry and use firearms on duty but must check their guns each night at Brink's. In emergencies they have aided police in apprehending criminals."

As an indication of how Brink's has responded in an emergency, one of many letters received after the bank holiday of 1933, described in Chapter VI, is quoted here:

> "To me, appreciation of one's efforts is worth more than monetary return.
>
> "Doing a cash business with large daily intakes and cash layouts, Kroger Company was peculiarly vulnerable to the inconvenience resulting from the bank moratoria beginning in Michigan and ultimately extending throughout the Nation.
>
> "I am not overstating the matter when I say that we could not have overcome, as we did, the difficulties thus presented without the assistance of your service. No matter how difficult or unforeseen the emergency, how much accuracy and responsibility it required, or how much unexpected effort was involved, you never hesitated nor slowed up on the job, nor questioned how you were to be compensated for the services performed.
>
> "The Kroger Company fully appreciates your co-operation and assistance and wishes you every success."

A file of thirty-nine letters received immediately after the Boston robbery testifies to the promptness with which Brink's has made good losses to customers. The tenor of all these letters is reflected in the following received from the president of the Navy Yard Employees Credit Union at the Naval Shipyard, Charlestown, Massachusetts.

"The Board of Directors wish to acknowledge with thanks your check for $63,000.00 which we received on Thursday Jan. 19, 1950 in payment for the money belonging to this Credit Union which was taken from your vaults at the time of the (Boston) robbery on Jan. 17, 1950. The promptness in which you paid this amount was amazing.

"The Board wishes also to thank you for the promptness in which your Boston, Mass. Office handled the situation on Jan. 18, 1950, in going to our bank and getting another supply of money and delivering to the Navy Yard, so that our service of cashing checks was not interrupted."

*   *   *

If founder Perry Brink could hear these praises, it would make him well satisfied with the seed he planted. Certainly there remains decidedly more than a trace of the Yankee canniness that prompted him to require his hired help to live in his own boarding house so that he could get back as profit some of the wages he paid out.

Reminiscent of this is an automobile license service offered in Chicago as a by-product of Brink's many "stops" and "runs" in the area. Licenses are picked up and delivered for currency exchanges and other retail outlets where applications are accepted.

The profit for Brink's? A very small sum per license. But Brink's of 1959 or of 1859—it's all the same—never passes up a chance to pick up an honest dollar. Keep this incentive alive in a company—moving a few trunks a day or a billion and a third dollars a day—and there is no need to worry about its continued healthy growth.

Chronological List of Brink's Services

Payroll Service
    Bulk Payroll Delivery 1891
    Put Up and Deliver. 1901
    Put Up, Deliver and Pay Off 1907

Pick Up and Deposit 1893

Bank Services 1900

Pick Up, Consolidate, Deposit 1917

Clearing House Service 1920

Check Cashing Service 1920

Safe Service 1925

Federal Reserve Service 1932

Parking Meter Service. 1949

United States Mint Service 1954

Chronological List of Brink's Offices

CHICAGO, ILL.
May 5, 1859

CLEVELAND, OHIO
July 1, 1918

ROCHESTER, N. Y.
January 1, 1920

NEW YORK, N. Y.
January 2, 1922

PHILADELPHIA, PA.
January 13, 1922

DETROIT, MICH.
January 1, 1923

NEWARK, N. J.
January 22, 1923

PROVIDENCE, R. I.
August 3, 1923

PITTSBURGH, PA.
January 1, 1924

WORCESTER, MASS.
February 1, 1924

SYRACUSE, N. Y.
February 20, 1924

ST. LOUIS, MO.
June 1, 1924

KANSAS CITY, MO.
June 3, 1924

MINNEAPOLIS, MINN.
November 1, 1924

TOLEDO, OHIO
June 1, 1925

BOSTON, MASS.
August 25, 1925

BUFFALO, N. Y.
December 1, 1925

NEW BEDFORD, MASS.
February 5, 1926

NEW HAVEN, CONN.
February 16, 1926

BALTIMORE, MD.
April 1, 1926

INDIANAPOLIS, IND.
December 3, 1926

LOS ANGELES, CAL.
January 2, 1927

WILMINGTON, DEL.
January 12, 1927

AKRON, OHIO
April 1, 1927

CINCINNATI, OHIO
May 19, 1927

GRAND RAPIDS, MICH.
August 1, 1927

SPRINGFIELD, MASS.
August 1, 1927

LOUISVILLE, KY.
August 11, 1927

DAYTON, OHIO
August 19, 1927

YOUNGSTOWN, OHIO
September 19, 1927

ERIE, PA.
September 21, 1927

FLINT, MICH.
October 1, 1927

COLUMBUS, OHIO
October 1, 1927

ATLANTA, GA.
June 1, 1928

ALBANY, N. Y.
January 9, 1929

PORTLAND, ME.
January 15, 1929

JOHNSTOWN, PA.
March 4, 1929

SOUTH BEND, IND.
April 1, 1929

UTICA, N. Y.
April 13, 1929

JACKSON, MICH.
June 1, 1929

KALAMAZOO, MICH.
June 1, 1929

LANSING, MICH.
June 1, 1929

BIRMINGHAM, ALA.
July 5, 1929
•
OKLAHOMA CITY,
OKLAHOMA
August 1, 1929
•
WASHINGTON, D.C.
December 2, 1929

FORT WAYNE, IND.
October 1, 1930

DAVENPORT, IOWA
February 12, 1931
•
PEORIA, ILL.
February 17, 1931
•
WICHITA, KAN.
December 1, 1931

SPRINGFIELD, ILL.
October 19, 1932

CANTON, OHIO
October 15, 1935
•
BINGHAMTON, N. Y.
November 1, 1935
•
NORFOLK, VA.
November 1, 1935
•
WILKES-BARRE, PA.
November 1, 1935
•
RICHMOND, VA.
November 1, 1935

EVANSVILLE, IND.
August 1, 1939

HAMMOND, IND.
March 1, 1940

ROCKFORD, ILL.
January 1, 1946
•
OAKLAND, CAL.
June 1, 1946
•
SAN FRANCISCO, CAL.
June 1, 1946

TOPEKA, KAN.
July 1, 1947
•
RALEIGH, N. C.
October 1, 1947
•
SAN BERNARDINO,
CALIFORNIA
October 1, 1947
•
MUSKEGON, MICH.
November 1, 1947
•
ST. JOSEPH, MO.
November 15, 1947

TERRE HAUTE, IND.
February 1, 1948
•
CEDAR RAPIDS, IOWA
February 1, 1948
•
MONTGOMERY, ALA.
May 3, 1948
•
JACKSONVILLE, FLA.
October 1, 1948
•
WHEELING, W. VA.
December 1, 1948
•
MUNCIE, IND.
December 30, 1948

SPRINGFIELD, OHIO
May 1, 1949

TAMPA, FLA.
February 10, 1953
•
WEST PALM BEACH,
FLORIDA
August 6, 1953
•
COLUMBUS, GA.
August 24, 1953

TULSA, OKLA.
December 1, 1954

DECATUR, ILL.
August 1, 1955
•
LYNCHBURG, VA.
October 1, 1955

SAGINAW, MICH.
May 1, 1956

LOWELL, MASS.
January 1, 1957
•
BROCKTON, MASS.
January 1, 1957
•
LANCASTER, CAL.
March 18, 1957
•
MANSFIELD, OHIO
September 3, 1957

GADSDEN, ALA.
June 1, 1958
•
EUREKA, CAL.
September 15, 1958
(continued)

Chronological List
of Brink's Subsidiary Companies

BRINK'S EXPRESS COMPANY OF CANADA, LIMITED

MONTREAL, QUE.
July 21, 1927

TORONTO, ONT.
February 1, 1928

WINNIPEG, MAN.
May 22, 1939

HAMILTON, ONT.
December 13, 1941

QUEBEC, QUE.
May 11, 1942

OTTAWA, ONT.
July 2, 1942

LONDON, ONT.
June 1, 1947

THREE RIVERS, QUE.
June 1, 1947

WINDSOR, ONT.
December 15, 1948

NIAGARA FALLS,
ONTARIO
December 14, 1953

REGINA, SASK.
July 1, 1954

SASKATOON, SASK.
February 1, 1955

HALIFAX, N.S.
July 4, 1955

PORT ARTHUR, ONT.
October 1, 1955

ST. JOHN, N.B.
July 2, 1956

PETERBOROUGH,
ONTARIO
July 14, 1958

SHERBROOKE, QUE.
February 2, 1959

BRINK'S, INCORPORATED OF WISCONSIN

MILWAUKEE, WIS.
September 19, 1927

MADISON, WIS.
December 9, 1940

BRINK'S, INCORPORATED OF TEXAS

HOUSTON, TEXAS
January 13, 1928

BEAUMONT, TEXAS
February 1, 1948

GALVESTON, TEXAS
March 15, 1948

BRINK'S EXPRESS COMPANY

CHICAGO, ILL.
November 16, 1930

SOUTHERN ARMORED SERVICE, INC.

LAKE WORTH, FLA.
November 1, 1957

ORLANDO, FLA.
November 1, 1957

DAYTONA BEACH, FLA.
November 1, 1957

TALLAHASSEE, FLA.
April 1, 1958